Shades of Expression

Online Political Journalism in the Post-Colour Revolution Nations

Shades of Expression

Online Political Journalism in the Post-Colour Revolution Nations

Simon Gwyn Roberts

University of Chester Press

First published 2013
by University of Chester Press
University of Chester
Parkgate Road
Chester CH1 4BJ

Printed and bound in the UK by the
LIS Print Unit
University of Chester
Cover designed by the
LIS Graphics Team
University of Chester

A catalogue record for this book is available from the
British Library

ISBN 978-1-908258-07-6

CONTENTS

LIST OF ILLUSTRATIONS

PREFACE

The Colour Revolutions in the former Soviet Union were the twenty-first century's first successful attempts to overthrow political elites through mass protest and civic society activism. They are of intrinsic interest to media scholars because concepts of media freedom were located at the heart of the protests against semi-autocratic post-Communist regimes and have continued to characterise political debate in Georgia, Ukraine and Kyrgyzstan. The ideals that underpinned the events were echoed several years later in the Arab world, and both initially involved influential networks of activists ranged against political elites. However, there was one critical difference in terms of media context: the events of the Arab Spring were often facilitated and given added impetus by the advances in news media technology which had taken place over the latter half of the decade and which allowed for more effective networked communications and a more open public sphere to thrive, even in autocratic environments. Indeed, Cheterian (2011) compares the role of new media in the Arab Spring to that of the printing press in the European revolutions of 1848.

But while the role of evolving media technologies has been extensively analysed and critiqued in the context of the Arab world, its use in the more mature post-Revolution environments of the former Soviet Union has been largely overlooked. Yet the very centrality of media freedom to the Colour Revolutions in Georgia, Ukraine and Kyrgyzstan – combined with structural deficiencies in the traditional news media and a longer experience of continuing political instability as those nations move towards varying degrees of democracy – renders the role of new media technology potentially highly revealing, and also contains salutary lessons for the younger post-revolution environments of Egypt and Tunisia.

The democratising role and potential of new media technology remains disputed in many global contexts, but Mason (2013) argued that the benefit of hindsight two years after the events of the Arab Spring allows for a clearer hypothesis, suggesting that a fundamental change has occurred, amounting to nothing less than a shift in human consciousness and behaviour revolving around the rise of the networked individual. New forms of media technology alter the balance of power in favour of those networked individuals, whose ability to challenge political elites in autocratic or semi-autocratic environments has increased substantially via more efficient and effective communication.

Whether this balance has shifted decisively is a moot point, but comparative analysis can reveal more about its potential. In many different global environments, the continuing economic crisis is leading to an interaction of social media and online journalism with a mainstream press that is, itself, undergoing rapid change. This book argues that the real scope of these evolving technologies during the economic downturn arguably lies in the development of news "hub" websites capable of acting as portals which mobilise a combination of social media, blogs and independent political journalism to plug a gap in the public sphere which cannot be filled by a deficient mainstream press fatally compromised by lack of funds.

The three post-Soviet Colour Revolutions that ultimately succeeded in deposing semi-autocratic regimes, characterised by varying degrees of corruption, in the early years of the twenty-first century all had distinctive contextual settings but shared some common features. All three followed disputed elections, and all were characterised by young people organising themselves into networks, using eye-catching slogans and non-violent action. Since the events took place, however, both the underpinning reasons for, and the long-term effects of, the Colour Revolutions have been questioned. Some argue that they were not the paradigm-shifting events they first appeared to be: rather, that they were merely further chapters in the evolution of post-Communist states and might serve as a warning (to those interpreting the significance of the Arab Spring, for example) not to conflate democratic breakthroughs with genuine democratisation. But such arguments lose some of their validity by ignoring the incremental, yet significant, changes to have occurred in recent years. Two obvious examples of these processes are the 2011–12 peaceful transitions of political power following elections in Georgia and Kyrgyzstan. Georgia's October 2012 election was the first democratic transfer of power in the country's post-Soviet history (Harding, 2012), while Kyrgyzstan's peaceful 2011 election led some to argue that it had become Central Asia's first Parliamentary democracy (Kilner, 2012).

ACKNOWLEDGEMENTS

This study was made possible by the award of a research grant by the University of Chester in 2011 to 2012.

With thanks to all participating journalists, Guy Hodgson, Vera Slavtcheva-Petkova, Brendan O'Sullivan, Morgan, Eve and Kate.

INTRODUCTION
THE LANDS OF THE "SEMI-FREE"

Studies examining the democratising potential of new media have tended towards a somewhat parochial Western Centrism, which has characterised much of the ensuing debate and therefore often failed to fully predict the effects in other contexts and cultures. While new media's role in circumventing the obviously deficient news media environment of parts of the Arab world attracted global attention *post*-Arab Spring, and some attempts have been made to examine the impact in other overtly authoritarian regimes, this book argues that the most revealing dynamic is elsewhere: in "West-facing" post-Soviet countries which embrace concepts of media freedom and democracy yet fail to fully implement them. In these media environments, sometimes described as "semi free" (Robakidze, 2011), web access is often very high, partly driven by the failures of the mainstream independent press to capitalise on the post-Communist environment combined with political in-stability and associated limitations on the freedom of the press.

Attempts to "de-Westernise" studies of journalism in a general sense have been made in recent years, with Curran and Park's 2000 study, for example, challenging some of the assumptions that have tended to characterise academic debate in the UK and US. More recently, the impact of internet-enabled communication in politics in autocratic or semi-autocratic regimes has been examined in a general sense, with research into authoritarian regimes' attempts to censor online content, for example (Deibert, Haraszti, Palfrey, Rohozinski & Zittrain, 2010). However, examina-tions of online journalism more specifically have tended

1

towards a rather Eurocentric default interpretative perspective. This is particularly true in terms of qualitative work that examines the role, opinions and experiences of journalists themselves, with genuinely comparative research from outside Europe and North America rather rare.

Four countries on similar contemporary political trajectories – Ukraine, Georgia, Kyrgyzstan and Armenia – are examined in this book. Georgia, Ukraine and Kyrgyzstan were the three former Soviet countries to experience so-called "Colour Revolutions" in the mid 2000s, with "media freedom" a fundamental part of protestor's demands during the demonstrations which led to the overthrow of incumbent post-Communist governments. The three events, Georgia's "Rose Revolution" in 2003, Ukraine's "Orange Revolution" in 2004 and Kyrgyzstan's "Tulip Revolution" in 2005, were considered by some – particularly those on the political right – to represent the continuation, or perhaps conclusion, of what political scientist Samuel Huntington described as the "third wave" of global democratisation (Huntington, 1991).

Interpretations of the events themselves, and their subsequent significance, remain varied and controversial. Some political analysts suggest that they were led primarily by US foreign policy, facilitated by US-sponsored NGOs (for example, Chaulia, 2006) and characterised by easily digested, PR-driven slogans, while others argue that they were spontaneous, indigenous expressions of dissatisfaction with post-Soviet regimes. These varied interpretations were later echoed by the debates that surrounded the events of the Arab Spring, whereby some commentators chose to view them as indigenous expressions of anger and desire for regime change, whilst others emphasised the role of Western media technologies in the coordination and facilitation of revolution. Indeed, the events of the Arab Spring mirrored the earlier post-Soviet Colour Revolutions in more fundamental ways as the "domino effect" of the protests spread to more and more countries. It briefly seemed possible to argue that the protests in North Africa and the Middle East represented direct successors to the Colour Revolutions and perhaps – taken together – encapsulated a "fourth wave" of global democratisation, at least partly based on conceptions of media freedom, notwithstanding the uncomfortable subsequent reality that in both environments the drift back to a form of autocracy was alarmingly swift in some countries. In this context, it is worth pointing out that former Kyrgyz President Roza Otunbayeva claimed the events of the Arab Spring were directly inspired by the subsequent 2010 revolution in Kyrgyzstan, which deposed President Kurmanbek Bakiev, and was extensively covered by Al Jazeera's global news network (Kilner, 2012).

If the origins and motives behind the Colour Revolutions remain disputed, one incontrovertible fact remains: they succeeded in challenging the post-Soviet political establishment through activism and (largely) peaceful demonstrations. Further, the three countries in which Colour Revolutions succeeded in removing governments have remained characterised by varying degrees of political liberalism and a continuing emphasis on media freedom as a desirable – if not guaranteed – feature of public life.

Some analysts argue that the fourth country examined in this book, Armenia, was the *first* post-Soviet country to experience such a process following the attempted overthrow of the government in 1996, and therefore a form of archetype for subsequent events elsewhere in the post-

Soviet world, although it did not undergo a full revolution at the time (Iskandaryan, 2005). Many of the ideals expressed during the Colour Revolutions, particularly those surrounding media freedom, continue to characterise debate in Armenia as they do in the three Post-Colour Revolution countries. Despite these similar political trajectories, however, the underpinning cultural, social and economic context differs considerably, with a comparative approach to the research revealing some significant areas of congruence whilst simultaneously stressing the importance of geopolitical context in the development and effectiveness of online journalism.

A series of immersive interviews with active online and mainstream journalists in all four countries, conducted in Tbilisi (Georgia), Kiev (Ukraine), Kharkov (Ukraine), Yerevan (Armenia) and Bishkek (Kyrgyzstan) between April 2011 and September 2012, forms the backbone of this work. The intention was to capture a "snapshot" of the contemporary role of online journalism in rapidly evolving post-Soviet, post-Colour Revolution political environments, exploring the wider journalistic and political context alongside the use and influence of online news sites. In particular, the book aims to fill a gap in the literature by undertaking qualitative work which explores the views of active journalists in the post-Colour Revolution nations and seeks to assess their views on the role and potential role of online political journalism in those environments. The book identifies one particularly significant recent factor in the development of online journalism as it affects the wider media and political environment in all four countries. This is the emergence of phenomena that might be best described as "hub websites", specialising in independent political journalism. Such sites often differentiate themselves from the standard Western version of web news portals by frequently sidestepping the mainstream press, and often marshalling an additional range of disparate web-based sources, including blogs and social media, around which an engaged and politically active population is coalescing.

CHAPTER 1

ONLINE POLITICAL JOURNALISM IN CONTEXT: BEYOND THE "ECHO CHAMBER"

The deficiencies of contemporary mainstream journalism generate political attention in many contexts and countries worldwide. Typically, critiques in Europe and North America revolve around structural problems and resource issues which combine with a commercial disinclination to cover politics to contribute to a "disconnect" between the processes of democracy and the voting public. In other contexts, the commercial disinclination to cover politics is sometimes replaced by rather more serious forms of direct or indirect censorship and other forms of control over the press. Beckett (2008) argues that the long-running debate about the gulf between the democratic ideal and the prevailing reality is increasingly situated in the news media itself. In a climate in which the democratic function of the news media is increasingly called into question, a parallel growth in the scope and ambition of political blogs, politically motivated social media and other forms of internet-enabled political communication is perhaps unsurprising, with several commentators arguing that the internet offers increased opportunities for enhanced democratic discourse.

Predictions that the internet will reinvigorate public debate and reconnect politicians to their public are not new: Blumler and Coleman called for a "civic commons in cyberspace" as early as 2001, and well before that the new media environment's implications for political communication was being explored by academics. Much of this early optimism about the potential of the internet to reinvigorate the public sphere subsequently faded, with commentators challenging the more extravagant claims and arguing that new media's democratising potential and impact on journalism had been exaggerated. Entrenched perspectives and polarised opinions then characterised the debate for several years, which led Agre (2002) to point out that the internet has its effect only in the ways that it is appropriated, and it is appropriated in so many different ways that nobody has enough information to add them up. More recently, Beckett (2008) rued the tendency to look at the post-internet journalism business from two extremes. One insists traditional journalism must be defended, the other is unrealistically evangelical about the potential of new media. As early as 2004, however, Gilmor rejected the polarised nature of this debate, which was often framed from the perspective of professional journalists expressing a fear of creeping amateurism. Instead, Gilmor argued there will be a mutually beneficial move towards an era of media literacy and what he called "news activism", whereby web technology allows people in various global contexts to regain control of the news. When people become more engaged with the events around them, particularly when they become journalistic activists, they become better citizens.

Gilmor's predictions now seem prescient: since the turn of the decade there have been numerous signs that the former polarity has dissolved into a more nuanced and arguably more realistic assessment of the significance of prevailing trends. A renewed optimism about the democratising potential of the web has crept back into public debate, with an acknowledgement that "citizen journalism" can be harnessed by professional journalists to produce new forms of political debate. For Beckett (2010), for example, the British General Election of 2010 made it "absolutely clear that networked journalism had arrived" and the renewed power of the network in the post-web global context has been assessed by Mason (2012) and others. Numerous further studies of convergence in the Western context have attempted to assess the relationship between news organisations and online media platforms, typically finding that connectivity implies a dramatic conceptual shift for journalists whereby readers frequently challenge journalists and sources. News organisations find that part of their mission includes hosting a user community that may not conform to journalistic norms, while social networks find that shared user-generated content is often akin to "news". For some, this interactivity represents the culmination of the populist promise of journalism, while for others it marks a dilution of journalistic expertise (Braun and Gillespie, 2011). In a broader, global context, Coleman and Blumler (2009) called for journalists to form a connection between citizens and "the confusing mass of online as well as offline information sources", with the World Economic Forum's global council calling for journalism to reconstruct its relationship with the citizen and society, arguing that public engagement is transforming journalism and providing a "historic opportunity to create unprecedented increased value" (World Economic Forum, 2009).

This renewed optimism seemed vindicated in early 2011, as developments in the Arab world brought many of these trends to global attention. The use of social media, political blogs and other forms of new media during the political unrest across the Arab world continues to be debated, with some arguing that online journalism facilitated protest and disseminated political information so effectively in Tunisia and Egypt, for example, that popular revolutions succeeded more rapidly than may otherwise have been the case (Filiu, 2011; Mason, 2012). Others doubted its efficacy and role in the political process, and indeed several writers (Markham, 2013, for example) were critical of the pseudo-Orientalist tendency of media academics to "project their own values" on to events in the Arab Spring. However, it remained a defining moment for the democratising potential of web-based media and net-worked journalism in a context which perfectly demon-strated its possibilities in terms of circumventing prevailing deficiencies in the mainstream press: associated, as they were in this case, with authoritarian regimes. In these "deficient" media environments, typified by parts of the Arab world, online media gained traction and impact in a way that is arguably impossible in the wider Anglosphere for commercial and structural reasons. In other words "big media", in these contexts, is too dominant: with the evi-dence suggesting that readers still coalesce around the websites of established media players (see, for example, Messner and DiStasto, 2008).

Prevailing conceptions of media models and effects have struggled to provide an analytical framework for recent global developments in online journalism, constrained as they still often are by an over-reliance on a limited, often rather one-dimensional Westerncentric worldview. There have, however, been several attempts to break free of the highly generalised global media models that characterised "Western" conceptions of journalistic approaches for many years. Siebert, Peterson and Schramm's (1956) *Four Theories of the Press*, for example, is often cited as the pre-eminent example of such a generalised model, with its broad global divisions: the "free world" of liberal democracy; the

"Soviet-Communist" sphere; and authoritarian societies typified by parts of the developing world and fascist regimes. This reductive overview argued that media systems merely reflect the prevailing philosophy and political system of the society in which they operate. Very much a product of its time, and a reflection of the era's geopolitical reality, echoes of the theory remain. Indeed, Curran and Park (2000) accuse the "four theories" model of establishing a convention that has stayed with us, in the sense that "lack of knowledge about other media systems need not get in the way of confident global generalization" (p. 6).

Instead, Curran and Park attempt to make the case for "de-Westernising" media studies and, by extension, reducing or removing both the tendency to regard the experience of the US and UK as typical, and the tendency to adopt a version of relativism when assessing the merits of non-Western media systems:

> We are not suggesting that normative values have only a zonal application. On the contrary, the values of liberty, equality and solidarity seem to us to have a universal validity. Our argument is that media studies will benefit from developing a wider comparative perspective. At the moment, ways of understanding the world's media system are unduly influenced by the experience of a few, untypical countries. These distort understanding not only of non-Western countries but also of a large part of the West as well" (Curran and Park, 2000, p. 15).

Similarly, Hallin and Mancini (2004) point out that much of the literature on the media is ethnocentric, *reading local contexts as if the model in one country were universal*. More recent attempts have been made to extend Hallin and

Mancini's frequently cited categorisation of media systems, thereby extending the scope of critical thinking on the subject, yet placing the post-Colour Revolution nations into such categories remains problematic. Because they tend to fall between different models, they neatly illustrate the dangers of generalisation, even when attempts have been made to adopt a more sophisticated approach to media models and categorisation. Critiques of the tendency to generalise revolve around analysis of the media in general, sometimes predating the widespread take-up of web-based technology, but Matheson (2009) argues that blogs are no different from the wider media and also need to be theorised in terms of their contexts. This seems something of an understatement. Indeed, it could be argued that online journalism (and, in particular, online political journalism) is considerably *more* contextually specific in terms of its role and impact.

Despite this, however, the problem of Westerncentric interpretations persists, with meaningful comparative work still surprisingly rare. Academic assessments of the democratising potential of online journalism in its broadest sense have sometimes been unhelpfully monocultural and pessimistic in their conclusions. Mason (2012), by contrast, argued that 2011 saw a revival of the essential appeal of the blogging format, and that the influence of that format was most clear in the Arab world, where the mainstream press have historically been subject to various degrees of censorship and self-censorship. For Mason, blogs exhibit a property that is vital "in theatres of revolution", by providing "somewhere to link to". They have come to resemble, in contexts blighted by a deficient mainstream media, the British newspapers of the nineteenth century: journals of record. Those journals of record are frequently able to gain a wider, global audience in the right circumstances, as the events of the Arab Spring demonstrated.

The influence of the media in general is particularly strong in countries where residents depend on a limited number of news sources, and weaker where there are multiple sources. In many post-Soviet countries, an independent mainstream press failed to fully develop, and newspaper circulations remain very low. As a result, the most influential web-based news websites gain a dual potential audience: a domestic audience seeking independent news and comment that cannot be provided by the mainstream press, and a foreign (often diasporic) audience seeking impartial information about political developments. Guy Berger (2009) argues that web technology means that a new form of global journalism is now possible, where local reporters' work is accessible online and the local becomes global.

Any theory of blogging's power therefore needs to account for differences in the cultural political context between the places in which it is used. Blogs do not conjure up an "instant free press" but place their authors in a more complex relationship to the norms and forces of social life (Matheson, 2009). The way knowledge is produced and understood in blogging in the US and Western Europe is a product of particular cultural circumstances: blogs emerge in this wider context and therefore reflect it. Blogs in Western cultures are not, for Matheson, reducible to conventional politics: they cannot be read simply as liberal democracy in action, nor evidence of a renewed public sphere, because they operate partly outside the institutions of politics and outside the values of public debate. Haas (2005) notes that politically orientated blogs in the US have tended to be "echo chambers" for existing elite sources of news and opinion and, indeed, this specific criticism has become a frequent refrain from observers of online journalism in both the US and UK. Several authors have also highlighted the tendency of blog commentaries to emphasise individual freedom; the implication is frequently critical, in that such an emphasis has limited explanatory or predictive power. Again, however, it is important to point out that such interpretations, although striving to place more emphasis on cultural context and global scope, still fall into a culturally specific trap. Outside the Anglosphere, or the wider Western world, blogs may perform very different functions: the "echo chamber" critique becomes less relevant, as indeed does the suggestion that they operate outside the values of public debate. Instead, online journalism in non-Western contexts begins to provide vital foci for engaging politically active members of the public: often supplanting a deficient, or barely existent, mainstream press in the process. It must also be conceded that there is a related, less positive tendency (apparent in post-Arab Spring North Africa, for example) for unlimited access to blogs and social media following several decades of censored news to generate new varieties of sometimes scurrilous opinionated journalism, where (for instance) conspiracy theories abound (A. Abrougui, personal communication, 5 April, 2012). In the post-Soviet context, rapidly evolving political environments such as Kyrgyzstan also encapsulate this tendency: blogs and other forms of web-based journalism were accused by several of those interviewed for this research of actively contributing to political instability by their reliance on rumour and opinion.

Such critiques run the risk of relativism, however, and have been thrown into sharper focus since the events of the Arab Spring. Implicit in such an analysis is the suggestion that applying established Western models of democracy to unstable political environments like Kyrgyzstan is postcolonial at root, inappropriate in the geopolitical context. But there must be a model of some sort, and Curran and Park's argument that liberty, equality and solidarity have a universal validity in the context of the media is arguably a more positive point of departure, whilst acknowledging that geopolitical context remains important. Indeed, even in the post-EU transitional democracies of Eastern Europe there is a continuing tendency to dissociate trust in media from trust in political institutions, for example, which contrasts sharply with more established Western European democracies (Lasas, 2013) and the interviews conducted for this book suggested that this distance is considerably greater in the post-Soviet context.

CHAPTER 2

DEFICIENT MEDIA ENVIRONMENTS: POST-SOVIET TRAJECTORIES IN GLOBAL CONTEXT

Some underpinning features of the modern media are now almost universal. The onset of communication abundance, characterised by multiple channels and the proliferation of communication devices has led to certain consequences, such as intensified competition for audience, associated pressures on journalists and politicians to adapt to the new resultant paradigm, increased populism and anti-elitist sentiment, increased diversity of agenda and opinion, and a mixture of fragmentation, flexibility and inadvertency in audience reception of politics (Blumler, 2012). However, although such trends are near universal, there remains a considerable gulf between the most seriously deficient *journalistic* environments, and those that remain characterised by a functioning and informative press. What might be described as deficient media environments, where journalistic ideals in terms of maintaining a healthy public sphere are far from realised, can be identified in very different and distinctive global contexts. At one end of the scale are overtly authoritarian regimes like those of the pre-2011 Arab world. But at the other, deficiencies can often be identified in unexpected contexts: not always those stereotypically associated with a problematic news media. For example, in devolved entities across the EU, media portrayal of devolved politics is often compromised for structural and economic reasons. Wales, for instance, a devolved entity within the structures of the UK government, has been described as "a media wasteland" (Davies, 2009) with no national newspaper press and an almost total dependence on London-based UK newspapers for political information. Cushion, Lewis and Groves (2009) argue that "English-centric assumptions about national identity" increasingly characterise UK national newspapers post-devolution, leading to a democratic deficit in other parts of the UK, where the nature of devolved governments and the increasingly distinctive policies they pursue are neither understood nor scrutinised. Instead, independent political websites have begun to gain traction. An important distinction should be drawn between conventional blogs and such sites, which transcend the blogging form, acting more like independent political news sites, and therefore become "hubs" for engaged readers by deliberately addressing the structural and economic deficiencies in the mainstream (Roberts, 2011).

This article argues that the emergence of dominant independent "hub" websites characterises contemporary online journalism in many different global contexts, but that this trend has remained relatively under-recognised by analysts who have either been overly preoccupied with the use of social media in authoritarian countries, or overly focused on the impact of conventional blogs in the Anglo-sphere (see, for example, the *Columbia Journalism Review's* "Future of Media" special report, 2012). Away from these environments, however, increasingly influential hub websites now shape political journalism in environments ranging from Wales (*WalesHome*) to Tunisia (*Nawaat.org*). Indeed, the overtly political *Nawaat.org* in Tunisia provided a neat encapsulation of the role of hub websites in relation to social media when it published a detailed story debunking what it called the "myth" of the "Twitter Revolution" in that country, concluding that social networks were neither the catalyst nor the organisational framework of the protest movement, and that the later Wikileaks reports about Tunisia did not change anything, as the public were already aware of regime corruption. Tunisian journalist Afef Abrougui argues that *Nawaat*'s impact as a collated source of semi-professional, determinedly independent journalism far outweighed that of individual blogs and social media (A. Abrougui, personal communication, 5 April 2012). Similarly, Markham (2013) suggests that media scholars and commentators have focused disproportionately on social media in their interpretation of the events of the Arab Spring. That is not to say that individual blogs do not have a role in some contexts and cultures. Examples are numerous, but to take one notable recent study, Khiabany and Srebeny (2009) analysed the role of blogs in the authoritarian context of Iran, finding that trade unions, women's movements and student groups are able to articulate their positions via such small-scale journalistic offerings: positions that are otherwise ignored by the mainstream, state-controlled media. Both citizenship and journalism are, they argue, experiencing a revival through innovative and alternative forms of expression that directly relates to the overarching authoritarian political context. The impact of small-scale blogs is magnified by that political context, although it remains limited by comparison to Abrougui's description of *Nawaat*'s role in post-Revolution Tunisia.

In this global, comparative context, this book will argue that the most revealing context in terms of the democratising potential of this kind of independent online journalism lies in that group of countries which occupy a middle ground between overtly authoritarian and censorship-dominated media environments (like Iran, where individual blogs may have a wider political impact), and those where commercial and structural factors are the main constraint on informed political journalism. Abrougui's post-Revolution Tunisian media is one such example, but this third group is perhaps best represented by the more nuanced news media environment characteristic of parts of the former Soviet Union.

Several former Soviet states present an intriguing and potentially revealing paradox in their approach to media freedom, and there are a number of reasons for this. Firstly, many of the states which gained independence from the Soviet Union in the 1990s have relatively small-scale mainstream media environments, frequently characterised by an almost non-existent contemporary print press and controversial TV ownership patterns, but also (as a partial consequence) have high levels of internet penetration, which is also assisted in several countries by relatively well-developed infrastructures. Related to this is an older newspaper reading tradition, inherited from Soviet times, which initially expressed itself in the form of a notable spike in readership in all four countries following independence and the birth of an independent, privately owned press. Secondly, several countries in the former Soviet Union have attempted to enshrine media freedom into their constitutions, often as an integral part of moves towards democratic systems of government and often related to the demands of protestors during the Colour Revolutions. The Soviet dissident practice of samizdat literature cannot be separated from this political process: with self-published work, often overtly political, reproduced and distributed by hand throughout the Communist years. Although most often Russian, many texts revolved around nationality and the recent folk and political memory of censorship continued to underpin debate in the post-Soviet era. Finally, however, those moves towards media freedom have frequently been compromised in many post-Soviet societies by regimes intent on reasserting some measure of control over the mainstream, traditional press. In this context, the demo-cratising potential of online journalism is most clear, and finds its expression in the development and increasing influence of hub websites covering political debate via independent journalism.

Hanitzsch et al. (2011) identified a bloc of post-Communist countries (Bulgaria and Romania in their study) which they argued formed part of a large and distinctive group in terms of journalistic culture. They called this group "peripheral Western", relatively close to Western journalism culture as generally practised in North America and Western Europe, but considerably removed from a third group of transitional democracies and de-veloping countries which included China, Egypt and Russia. However, the deliberately limited, "broad-brush" nature of this study, which sampled several countries within each broad journalistic culture, obscures some of the complexities of post-Communist development.

For example, several post-Soviet societies, Ukraine and Georgia in particular, could be argued to currently sit somewhere between Hanitzsch et al.'s peripheral Western group exemplified by Bulgaria and Romania, and the transitional democracies group exemplified by Russia and China. Importantly, Hanitzsch et al. found that journalists who have to manage in a political climate that is relatively hostile to press freedom and democracy exhibit smaller power distance: political factors are, in other words, particularly pertinent to journalists' perceptions of media roles. This positioning is significant for the political trajectories of Ukraine, Armenia and Georgia in particular, because Splichal and Sparks (1994) argued that after the collapse of socialist regimes in the 1980s and 90s, Eastern European countries were largely caught up in imitating Western European practices in economy and politics. Countries like Bulgaria, Romania and Slovenia all sought membership of the European Union and modelled their democratic structures and media systems accordingly.

To an extent, this earlier experience illustrates the nature of the balancing act currently being undertaken further east in Ukraine, Armenia and Georgia: all three countries are "West-facing", with an occasionally explicit, frequently implicit long-term political aspiration to join the EU, yet simultaneously exhibiting a *realpolitik* tendency for political elites to attempt to manage the news media. All three countries are members of the Eastern Partnership of the EU (inaugurated in 2009) as well as the European Neighbour-hood Policy, which is intended to bind countries to the East and South of the present EU more closely to the Union itself. The Neighbourhood Policy offers a degree of finan-cial assistance and "the promise" of eventual membership. In return, the association agreement is supposed to be in-cumbent on human rights guarantees, trade reform and the like. The Eastern Partnership, meanwhile, in its entirety encompasses what the EU calls the six post-Soviet states of "strategic importance". These include Belarus, Azerbaijan and Moldova in addition to the three countries covered in this study. The Partnership emphasises trade relations, but also stresses the promotion of human rights, democracy and the rule of law (European Commission, 2009).

Belarus, Azerbaijan and Moldova all have poor human rights records, and record scores well below those of Armenia, Georgia and Ukraine in relation to media freedom (Freedom House, 2012). There are many contrasts in terms of media liberality, but perhaps the most notable is that the internet is tightly controlled in Belarus, Azerbaijan and Moldova. For example, Pearce and Kendzior (2012) argued that digital media is used for a form of "networked authoritarianism" in several former Soviet states, with the manipulation of digitally mediated social networks typically used more often than outright censorship: although the Azerbaijan government, for example, actively dissuades internet users from political campaigning.

All these countries were among the fifteen former Republics of the Soviet Union to begin a transition towards independence based on a market economy and some form of democracy in 1991. In the sphere of media law, many post-Soviet states abolished political censorship and sought to guarantee a measure of freedom of information, transforming a relationship of subordination of the media to political power which had lasted for more than seventy years (McNair, 2001). As evidenced by the work of Pearce and Kendzior (2012) in the Azeri context, however, the fifteen states have all experienced different paces and trajectories of change: the Baltic States are now fully functioning members of the EU, while some Central Asian countries remain characterised by authoritarianism. It is possible to identify some broad groupings of countries, however. The Baltic States are an obvious example of one such coherent grouping, and it could also be argued that Ukraine and Georgia have experienced *similar* political trajectories since the break-up of the Soviet Union and are therefore ripe for comparative study. Both experienced so-called "Colour Revolutions" in 2003 and 2004, with media freedom seen as one of the significant gains resulting from 2004's "Orange Revolution" (Ukraine) and 2003's "Rose

Revolution" (Georgia). However, there has remained a tension between the need to reform the press (as "media freedom" is intrinsically linked with democratic forms of government) and the desire to retain, or reinstate, some form of state control. The dynamic is intriguing and potentially reveals a wider truth about the democratising potential of new media in what Robakidze (2011) describes as "semi-free" media environments: those which partially embrace media freedoms yet fail to fully implement them. The so-called "Tulip Revolution", which took place in Kyrgyzstan in 2005, was the third and final "successful" Colour Revolution to have taken place in the former Soviet Union, and Kyrgyzstan's location – much further East in Central Asia – and markedly different cultural and economic context, combined with a turbulent recent political history and consequent high levels of political engagement (and relatively high levels of internet access) makes it arguably the most interesting and revealing of the countries considered here.

The descriptor "Colour Revolutions" is generally taken to describe as a single phenomenon a number of non-violent protests that succeeded in overthrowing regimes that were characterised by various degrees of authoritarianism and corruption during the first half of the twenty-first century (O'Beachain and Polese, 2010). It has tended to encompass post-Communist (indeed, largely post-Soviet) countries, with Georgia and Ukraine the highest profile, though similar movements for change have been seen in various other contexts (although, as in parts of the Arab world during 2011, protests have not always followed the peaceful model). All, however, can be summarised as attempts to challenge political elites through mass protest and civil society activism.

The long-term effects of the Colour Revolutions has been questioned, with Mitchell (2012), for example, arguing that they were not the paradigm-shifting events they first appeared to be. Rather, they were merely further chapters in the evolution of post-Communist states and, furthermore, serve as a warning (to those interpreting the significance of the Arab Spring, for example) not to conflate democratic breakthroughs with genuine democratisation. However, such arguments – which attempt to set the Colour Revolutions in a broader historical context – lose some of their validity by ignoring the incremental, yet significant, changes to have occurred in recent years. Two obvious examples of these processes are the 2011–12 peaceful transitions of political power following elections in Georgia and Kyrgyzstan. Similarly, the political gulf between present-day Georgia, Ukraine and Kyrgyzstan and, for instance, Azerbaijan, Belarus and Uzbekistan cannot be overstated.

There are two prevalent theoretical explanations for the origins of the Colour Revolutions in the former Soviet Union. The more common "geopolitical" analysis sees them as part of a wider political "conflict" between the West and Russia: the ultimate motive being the emergence of a pro-EU/US perspective, at least in ideological terms, in the non-Russian, post-Soviet world. Depending on one's political perspective this either represents a struggle for liberty and democracy, or a reflection of Western neo-imperialism. The second analytical response is "internal" or "systemic", which sees the Colour Revolutions as almost inevitable consequences of certain features of the political systems and political culture present in "transitional" societies and exemplified by some former Soviet societies (Zolyan, 2010).

Neither ·analysis is strictly true. The "geopolitical" analysis reflects the reality that both the "West" and Russia influenced the Colour Revolutions in both Georgia and Ukraine, but tends to overplay the influence of the EU and US. Rather, it could be argued that the "internal" model captures the more profound causes that lay behind them. Indeed, although it did not experience a full "revolution" during the 2000s, Zolyan (2010) argues that the Armenian case shows that the emergence of conditions that contain the potential for a "Colour Revolution" is a *consequence* of certain features of the political system that existed (and still exists) in some post-Soviet states. Such arguments suggest that there is an inherent connection between the peculiarities of the post-Soviet political system and the emergence of the pattern of Colour Revolutions (Zolyan, 2010, Mitchell, 2012). The example of Kyrgyzstan, which will be discussed in more detail later in the book, arguably relates even more clearly to the "internal" model, in which the worst features of the post-Soviet state (kleptocracy, corruption, poverty) almost inevitably contributed to instability and dissatisfaction with the ruling regime.

In terms of the rationale behind the comparative approach taken in this book, Hale (2005) argues that the "peculiarities" inherent in the post-Soviet political system that makes countries particularly likely to experience Colour Revolutions combine a democratic façade, including a formally democratic legal and institutional framework, with authoritarian mechanisms of decision-making and elite recruitment. Whilst many of the deficiencies inherent in the post-Soviet regimes of Ukraine, Armenia, Kyrgyzstan and Georgia have been addressed over the years since the Colour Revolutions, systemic problems remain, although these vary in their magnitude and political effect. Georgia and Ukraine were arguably the most significant examples of the wave of post-Soviet Colour Revolutions and were certainly the highest profile internationally, largely because the political histories of both countries were fundamentally changed by the protests, even if this stopped short of full democratisation. Since the Colour Revolutions in Ukraine and Georgia, both societies have been characterised by similar political trajectories, with an ongoing tension between democratising, EU-facing elements and a still extant Soviet mentality within the body politic.

Armenia, by contrast, has been largely overlooked in the analytical literature on Colour Revolutions (Zolyan, 2010). Whilst it is true that it did not experience a change of government through peaceful mass protests, attempted revolutions did take place and now Armenia offers a particularly interesting case study for the democratising potential of new media because its print press has declined even more dramatically than that of Ukraine and Georgia in the past five years. In addition, Armenian television tends to be dominated by Russian imports, and it remains considerably closer in cultural terms to Russia than its neighbour Georgia. As a partial result, Armenia has an unusually vibrant range of online news providers, some of which attract significant audiences. At the broader political level, whilst the Armenian government has a close relationship with Russia, it also looks westward.

Kyrgyzstan remains something of an exception, despite the fact that it is bracketed with Georgia and Ukraine as the third country to have indisputably undergone a peaceful change of government through civic pressure in the mid 2000s. Its location and subsequent (2005 onwards) history – far more turbulent than Ukraine, and more turbulent even than Georgia and Armenia – makes it an intriguing case study. Its location and related geopolitical situation, surrounded as it is by long-term authoritarian regimes like Uzbekistan and China, means that it is harder to generalise about the democratising potential of new media in Kyrgyzstan than in the other three countries considered here. It remains, by some distance, the most "liberal" country in Central Asia, however.

So while the political trajectories of all four countries may be similar, they are far from identical, and the cultural and geopolitical context remains highly distinctive. To illustrate the long-term importance of these varying political trajectories in terms of the development of media and political freedoms, and as a corrective to the views of Mitchell (2012) and others who question the long-term significance of the Colour Revolutions, post-Soviet independent countries that did not experience Colour Revolutions have generally engaged in varied examples of containment strategies. The three countries previously mentioned – Azerbaijan, Belarus and Moldova – are good examples of what the evolution of such "containment strategies" means to the functioning of an independent media. In Russia, too, the political elite appropriated the tactics of the Colour Revolutions by establishing a pro-regime youth movement called *Nashi*. This echoed Ukraine's Orange Revolution in its use of easily digested red-and-white symbolism but subverted the underpinning rationale. In Uzbekistan, which borders Kyrgyzstan in Central Asia, the containment strategy was more direct, sometimes involving a brutal repression of activists which followed the Stalinist maxim: liquidate the person and you liquidate the problem (Fumagalli and Tordjman, 2010). Indeed, Uzbekistan's President Karimov has publicly argued for what he calls "Eastern democracy", suggesting that Western news values and independence of the mass media are not appropriate for countries where there is "strong and enduring" respect for authority. In short, in countries engaging in such containment strategies individual liberties and press freedom should not extend beyond what is required to achieve economic development and national security (Shafer and Freedman, 2003).

Similarly, during the "Arab awakenings", the regimes in Syria, Bahrain and Libya adopted a hardline approach to contain the demands of activists after revolutions in Tunisia and Egypt had succeeded in deposing authoritarian rulers. In media terms, these containment strategies express themselves in terms of a refusal to adopt standard practices associated with "media freedom". However, Mason (2012) is more "globally" optimistic in his claims that what characterises *all* the recent Arab uprisings is the power of the network to defeat elites, and that those networks are now driven and facilitated by media technology (an evolution of the NGO-facilitated "networks" that drove the Colour Revolutions).

Comparative approaches also have obvious potential for revealing some significant areas of congruence whilst simultaneously stressing the importance of geopolitical context in the development and democratising potential of online journalism. The nature, role, philosophy and conception of journalism itself varies considerably around the world, although genuinely comparative research on journalism remains rare, particularly if that research involves more than two or three cultures (Hanitzsch, 2008). This is surprising, as comparative research is an obvious strategy for attempting to assess the role and function of journalism across cultural boundaries. Hanitzsch et al.'s (2011) comparative study of journalism cultures suggests that aspects of interventionism, objectivism and the separation of facts and opinion differ, sometimes quite considerably. In very general terms, the study found Western journalists less supportive of the active promotion of particular values, ideas and social change, and more likely to adhere to universal ethical principles. However, even this tentative attempt at a comparative generalisation might be disputed by those familiar with the output of British tabloids, to take just one "Western" example. The study also found that journalists from non-Western countries are generally more interventionist and more flexible in their ethical views, with the active promotion of values and ideas more common in developing societies and "transitional contexts".

The perceived sanctity of the "Anglo-American" or Western model cannot easily be subsumed into a consideration of the democratising potential of online journalism. Almost by definition, online forms of journalism are less insular and more open to the influences of other forms of journalism: these may be adapted to fit local circumstances or merged with practices imported from elsewhere. Indeed, Seib argued in 2002 for a form of "global journalism" as an alternative to the Anglo-American model, which requires journalists to understand how the links between countries affect one another in terms of politics, culture and economics. This global journalism requires an openness through which new information is absorbed and understood, unlike the Anglo-American liberal model which is characterised by a predetermined set of norms in which journalists seek to reconcile news narratives (Smith and McConville, 2011). Indeed, Fielden's 2012 comparative study of International Press Councils identified the challenges shared by regulators in an era marked by the blurring of boundaries between converging media platforms, between professional and citizen journalists and between national and global publication. The solution to such regulatory challenges perhaps lies in the sorts of open journalistic models which chime with the multi-faceted and open information approach adopted by the hub websites beginning to shape political debate in Ukraine, Armenia, Kyrgyzstan and Georgia.

CHAPTER 3

DEFINING TERMS: IDEALISED BENCHMARKS OF
JOURNALISTIC FUNCTION

This model may represent a tempting characterisation of the open online journalistic approach emerging in the post-Colour Revolution nations, but any discussion of the democratising potential of online journalism in deficient media environments must acknowledge the inevitable problems of methodological definition: what standards of democratisation is the study measuring both existing and potential future political journalism *against*? This is a difficult issue, and one that is of particular relevance in the post-Soviet environment, yet it is frequently marginalised in comparative studies. The three classical arguments for press freedom revolve around self-expression, truth seeking and the creation of a functioning public sphere. The most persuasive of these is, for O'Neill (2012), the latter: that our social, cultural and political life needs media communication that is not only accessible and intelligent but can be assessed for its reliability and provenance. Louw (2010) outlines the empiricist understanding of the world which underpins the ideals of "objective journalism" still frequently fetishised by liberal democracies. This suggests that objective news exists "out there" in the real world independent of the news media, whose job it is to find and record it objectively. Further, journalists are expected to eliminate their own subjectivity by applying journalistic formulas. However, this model has long been disputed by those who argue that journalists frequently construct the news rather than reflect it. (Tuchman, 1978). In other words, rather than performing the traditional idealised democratic function of empirically recording objective political news, journalists often obfuscate the political process by actively involving themselves in it. Such debates render a feasible, practical and contemporary definition of journalism's potential democratic role elusive.

Stromback (2006) goes some way to addressing this issue in a slightly wider context, arguing that much literature discussing the impact of media and journalism on democracy is critical of its effects on "democracy" but that it frequently fails to identify news standards by which the quality of news journalism might be evaluated. Some form of empirical approach is clearly required if this issue is to be addressed with any clarity, particularly in the context of post-Soviet countries like Georgia, Armenia, Kyrgyzstan and Ukraine, emerging from decades of authoritarian control and attempting to negotiate a route through democratisation and associated conceptions of media freedom. Few models specify with sufficient clarity the model of democracy to be used in normative departure, and suggest that the question of proper news standards cannot be addressed in isolation from the question of different normative models of democracy. For Stromback, it is only by specifying what kind of democracy we are referring to when using the term, and by specifying its normative implications for media and journalism, that we can fully understand how media and journalism affect democracy. It follows that it is not valid to claim journalism undermines or contributes to democracy per se.

This is a particularly pertinent, and awkward, issue in the post-Soviet environments considered here, where constitutional definitions are "young" and remain disputed following the Colour Revolutions and subsequent political upheavals and governmental change. Kyrgyzstan, for example, has experienced frequent political upheavals, up to and including full revolution, *since* its Colour (Tulip) Revolution of 2005. As a result, its constitution, and political system, has remained in an almost constant state of flux. Therefore, with reference to the views of Stromback, it is almost impossible to measure news media's "effects" on democracy on such post-Soviet environments, as defining a precise "normative" model of democracy would, in these contexts, be unhelpfully imprecise and contentious. Even in the somewhat more evolved and comparatively stable political environment of Georgia, for example, a highly significant long-term move from Presidential to Parliamentary democracy was taking place during the period within which this book was written.

As a result of such definitional difficulties, this work seeks instead to provide a "snapshot" of online journalism's potential in post-Soviet environments: the fact that normative definitions are problematic is, in a sense, the point of departure for this research. The intention is to assess what journalists themselves see as the potential role for online journalism in emerging democratic environments, even if the normative definitions of democracy within those countries is problematised by the flux associated with post-revolutionary environments. Public interest was referenced as an alternative, deliberately idealised "yardstick" of journalistic function, and the closest meaningful point of normative departure for subsequent discussions about the role of online journalism in these rapidly evolving political environments. This study aims instead for a richer contextual analysis based on interviews, an approach explored in more depth in Chapter 5.

The wider question of role conceptions remains deeply relevant to the study, even if precise definitions are problematised by the overarching political environment. If differing perceptions about the nature and role of journalism are rooted in divergent political systems, as well as historical and cultural traditions, they remain broadly reflected in what Hachten and Scotton (2007) call the five political concepts of the press found in the world today – authoritarian, Western, Communist, revolutionary, developmental. Although there are echoes of Siebert, Peterson and Schramm's much-criticised "Four Theories of the Press" model here, unlike that model, which argued that the press merely reflected political context, these are normative concepts that reflect how the media might theoretically per-form under certain political conditions and social values. An understanding of these contrasting approaches to the role and function of transnational journalism can help to clarify some of the issues that divide the world's press:

> All press systems exist somewhere along a continuum, from complete controls (absolute authoritarianism) at one end to no control (pure libertarianism) at the other. Absolute freedom of expression is a myth. Beyond that controls on the press are so varied and complex that it is difficult, if not impossible, to compare press freedom in one nation with that in another. In one country, newspapers may be under harsh, arbitrary political restraints; in another, they may be under more subtle, yet real, economic and corporate restrictions (Hachten and Scotton, 2007, p. 26).

The attempts by US-based Freedom House to apply an index of Press Freedom illustrate this "difficulty": the index can only be seen as an arbitrary attempt at a meaningful comparison. The index is sometimes quoted in this volume, largely because it remains one of the few sources of comparative information on the subject, although it was regarded as "politicised" by several of the participants in the research.

The relationship between democracy and journalism has been described as a social contract (Locke, 1966). But although journalism is based on democratic values, it can thrive with or without democracy: its crucial role, regardless of context, is in facilitating association, the coming together of people for a common purpose (Papacharissi, 2009). There is a certain amount of idealism inherent in definitions which suggest that journalism requires democracy as it is the only form of government that respects freedom of speech, expression and information. By respecting these freedoms, democracy fulfils its part of the contract, but it also requires a system for the flow of information, to facilitate public discussion and perform a watchdog function (Habermas, 1989). Returning to the views of Stromback (2006), defining precisely what this obligation means is problematic and almost inevitably controversial: what kind of information do the public need? Indeed, following the events of the Arab Spring several commentators pointed out the challenge of establishing what is meant by free speech in post-Mubarak Egypt, referencing the problem of how to distinguish between vitriol and violence, for example (Sakr, 2013). Several of the Kyrgyz participants in this study made similar points. However, even in the broader context of post-Soviet journalism, there is a certain definitional paradox: on the one hand journalism is often criticised for its content and negative effects on some aspects of democracy. On the other, critics are often not clear about which democratic standard they are applying when they criticise the media. It is one thing to argue that the media contributes to political cynicism and lack of engagement, quite another to specify why and how this might harm democracy. The arguments of Franklin (1997) and McNair (2000) encapsulate this debate further. Indeed, in the British context the role of journalism in the political process has been a topic of public debate and a focus of political struggle since the advent of the print media itself (McNair, 2000), with debate about the media's role in politics merely intensifying over time – perhaps reaching a climax with the Leveson Inquiry of 2012. McNair takes issue with what he calls the prevailing orthodoxy that we are living in a time of crisis, what Blumler and Gurevitch (1995) called a "crisis of public communication". This orthodoxy suggests that, although we live in a time communication plenty, we are actually starved of the information we need to function politically and perform our civic duties, because our media is primarily shaped by profit motives rather than those of civic duty. This echoes the views of Franklin, for whom contemporary journalism (in the UK at least) increases cynicism and detachment. McNair, however, argues that popular forms of journalism, like British tabloids, increase engagement and perform a useful democratic function despite the shortcomings of their style of reportage. Such debates also take place away from the Anglosphere, of course, yet frequently these issues remain framed from a distinctive Western perspective which does not assist their application in other environments, particularly those where concepts of democracy are rapidly evolving in conjunction with developments in media technology which facilitate a more open public sphere.

Even defining "political journalism" is increasingly difficult in both Western and non-Western contexts, because it has long been apparent that political journalism happens not just in and around the national legislature but in a variety of other political, or semi-political, fields (Tunstall, 1971). These semi-political fields have become even more important in recent decades, with finance and business, for example, extensively covered in both the US and UK, and (for example) Ukraine. This is largely because of the significant movement in the location of power, and in particular the dominance of the financial markets, despite the fact that less coverage of national legislature is frequently linked to accusations of "dumbing down".

In post-Soviet environments like those of Ukraine, Georgia, Kyrgyzstan and Armenia, political journalism in its most fundamental form has evolved in a distinctive way. After the collapse of Communism, numerous newspapers were founded in all four countries, but most failed to make a long-term impact partly due to the fact that the style of reportage continued to echo, stylistically, Soviet journalism. The development of a "commercial" media in the post-Soviet environment illustrates the problems inherent in a reductive interpretation of traditional media models or an acceptance of a simple causal relationship between political context and the wider media. The fall of Communism represented another major challenge to the ways in which we think about the media in general, and political journalism in particular, with Sparks (2000) citing an overly simplistic characterisation of the opposition of free market and state direction: a characterisation which still retains a paradigmatic status. While this polarity "tells us something true and important about the mass media (in that) there really is a difference between the ways in which the market shapes the media and the ways in which the state shapes the media" (p. 37), Sparks argues that this basic insight leads to a largely sterile debate about the value or otherwise of state intervention in mass media, that has tended to obscure any real analysis of the ways in which the media actually function with regard to social power. Instead, Communism's collapse made it clear that the fundamental opposition, in terms of the mass media fulfilling a role of informing the citizens of a state about its government, is not necessarily between commercial media and political media. Rather, these two forces may sometimes conflict, but may equally often act in concert. For Sparks, they both follow an essential logic that places them on the side of power. The phenomenon of close links between political and economic actors in the context of the news media is not peculiar to post-Communist societies, of course. Indeed, it could be argued to approach a global norm, particularly when one considers the role of Silvio Berlusconi in Italy, or the links between Rupert Murdoch's press empire and the British political establishment revealed by the Leveson Inquiry.

In this context, the revitalising impact of online journalism is potentially magnified: and that impact may be felt in a variety of different political contexts. Claims that there is a new confidence in mainstream journalism partly stimulated by engagement with online journalism and user-generated content are lent further clarity by the more recent views of Beckett (2010) and Mason (2012) which suggest a new kind of networked journalism is emerging where news media engages with audiences to tell stories in new ways, and that those stories are subsequently amplified by user engagement. Online news websites may function as virtual public spheres as they can be interconnected through online networks, enabling citizens to share a wide variety of information and news, participate in online discussions and build social networks (Dahlgren, 2005). Habermas's public sphere concept (1989) stresses open interaction and open communication as crucial features of democratic society: it follows that the interactivity and openness inherent in hub websites like the Georgian *Liberali* contribute to a public sphere hosting democratic forms of discourse. Through post-Soviet hub websites like *Liberali* and *Ukrainska Pravda*, citizens may interact with professional and citizen journalists, build networks and form perceived role conceptions of journalists. In this process, social trust among people in local communities and media credibility may play crucial roles when online news users perceive the roles of professional and citizen journalists as community members. In other words, perceptions of journalistic role conceptions may be influenced by the level of social trust and media credibility ascribed to news media and news content (Nah and Chung, 2012). In the hub websites emerging in the post-Colour Revolution nations, this trust expresses itself in a strong sense of "community engagement", heightened by the deficiencies of the mainstream press.

In emerging democracies like those of the post-Soviet world, the issue of defining standards of democracy is often clearer cut, partly because constitutional moves towards such definitions are much more recent: indeed, clarifying the relationship between the news media and democracy was core to the Colour Revolutions of 2003, 2004 and 2005. Fielden's study (2012) argues that, however press regulation is developed, in whatever context, the *interests of the public should lie at its heart.*

For the purposes of this work, an attempt was made to assess interviewees' views on this key theme in particular: it underpins the methodological approach outlined in

Chapter 5. Such considerations led to discussions about the democratising potential of online journalism in all four countries, and inevitably, progressed to a consideration of the wider democratic implications of such "open" forms of journalism as those pursued by hub websites. Public interest was then referenced as the idealised "yardstick" of journalistic function: the point of normative departure for all subsequent debates about the democratising role of online journalism in such rapidly evolving political environments.

CHAPTER 4

POST-COLOUR REVOLUTION
COUNTRY OVERVIEWS

There was, in the West, a tendency to generalise about media systems in the Eastern bloc during the Communist era, and in its immediate aftermath. This tendency remains, albeit in a watered down form, and illustrates a wider truth about the reliance of many Western observers on reductive interpretations of present-day media systems in parts of the former Soviet Union: interpretations that often suffer from a form of historical hangover from the Soviet era. It could be argued that this leads to a form of relativism, where Caucasian and Central Asian countries, in particular, re-moved by geography from the European mainstream, are "not expected" to have fully functioning democratically accountable media systems. Sparks (2000) attempted to put forward a corrective to such generalised attitudes when he cited the "very considerable degree of freedom" enjoyed in parts of Communist Eastern Europe in the 1970s and 1980s, although he also concedes that some systems had a greater "natural insulation" through language or geography. Certainly, there never was a single monolithic Communist media system.

Similarly, as this research attempts to demonstrate, present-day policies and broader ideological approaches to the media vary markedly across the post-Soviet world: fundamentally, a reflection of diverse political systems. But although the Post-Colour Revolution nations are charac-terised by their liberal approach to media freedom, relative to other parts of the former Soviet Union, their systems have sometimes been described as "managed democracy" and criticised as ultimately unsustainable, since they contain an inherent contradiction between a democratic façade and essentially authoritarian mechanisms of decision-making (Zolyan, 2010). In media terms, this expresses itself in an uneasy relationship between the State and an independent press and broadcast sector. Armenia, for example, has long been criticised for exhibiting some of these traits, and Yanukovych's Ukraine found itself accused of similar tendencies in 2011 (Shapovalova, 2011).

However, the majority of the newly independent post-Soviet States initially experimented with forms of managed democracy, before moving in two broadly diverging directions. One group of countries moved towards openly authoritarian regimes (Turkmenistan, Uzbekistan and Azerbaijan, for example) which tends to ensure stability at the expense of pluralism and liberty, while another group (arguably exemplified by Georgia, but including all four countries examined in this book) moved towards the creation of functioning democratic institutions, with varying degrees of media freedom contributing to wider mechanisms of public involvement and political decision-making.

However, despite such moves, none of the post-Colour Revolution nations scores very highly on the Human Development Index, which takes various indices relating to education, life expectancy and income to produce a global ranking. In 2011, Georgia ranked 75th, continuing an upward trend, Ukraine dropped to 77th, Armenia was ranked 87th and Kyrgyzstan 126th from 177 countries (United Nations Development Programme, 2012). In terms of media freedom, however, all four do better, as outlined at the end of this chapter.

Georgia

Present-day Georgia is, like Ukraine, a multiparty democracy with a clear commitment to a free press, but, like Ukraine, it still fails to fully achieve its idealistic aims of linking the two. Georgia gained independence from the Soviet Union in 1991, and like many other post-Soviet states it experienced a series of political and economic crises throughout the 1990s. The Georgian state under its first President, Eduard Shevardnadze was weak, rather than overtly authoritarian or liberal (Companjen, 2010). However, despite the widespread poverty and political failure associated with this "weakness", it was the closure of the independent TV station Rustavi 2 in 2001 that

triggered the largest protests against the Shevardnadze regime (Companjen, 2010). Media issues were thus at the heart of the debate about Georgia's democratic progress from the beginning, and have remained a key issue characterising political debate in the country.

Post-Soviet civil society in Georgia was initially stimulated through foreign organisations like the Soros Foundation, in which NGOs became a serious force in Georgian society and still fund several of the independent news websites

Figure 1. News-stand in Tbilisi, Georgia.

cited by interviewees and discussed later in this book. The alliance of NGOs, reformist politicians and independent media formed a catalyst for the "Rose Revolution" that followed the allegedly rigged elections of November 2003. For De Waal (2010) the revolution of 2003 "briefly electrified the world", as a rare example of popular democracy in action and a compelling spectacle "pulled off with Georgian flair" (p. 193). It was also the first of the Colour Revolutions that later removed presidents in Ukraine and Kyrgyzstan. Events were highly improvised and spontaneous and derived very largely from the miscalculations of President Shevardnadze, despite Russian-led accusations that the revolutions were planned with US assistance (De Waal, 2010).

After the "Rose Revolution", Robakidze (2011) says that "everybody believed, but only for a while, that journalism should be serving truth and providing objective information to citizens". Indeed, in 2004 Georgia adopted a new law "on freedom of speech and expression" which enshrines various media freedom principles within the constitution. Implementation proved more of a problem, and gradually the government strengthened its grip on TV media in particular. Print media enjoys more freedom, but circulation is very low and its influence limited.

Authoritarian hints were present from the beginning of the Saakashvili regime. He stripped Parliament of much of its powers and increased government control over TV stations as he turned Georgia from a semi-Parliamentary republic into a strongly Presidential one (Companjen, 2010). As early as 2004 a group of civil society activists chided the President for being intolerant of criticism and a Council of Europe report concluded the media was self-censoring and civil society weak. It could also be argued that the EU has been too cautious in Georgia, partly because it feels it should show a greater commitment to democracy and reform before increasing its engagement (De Waal, 2010).

The ideals behind the Rose Revolution were soon further compromised, with Robakidze (2011) arguing that much of the "media freedom" touted by President Saakashvili was simply rhetoric designed to boost his association with US and EU. The post-Soviet media legacy has been problematic in Georgia, with state interventions, unclear ownership – and perhaps most importantly difficult access to public information and broadcast licenses. Saakashvili initially successfully transformed the economy, targeting endemic corruption and reforming many state institutions. Perhaps even more significantly, he travelled widely and courted the Western media, winning positive profiles portraying Georgia as a democratic success story (De Waal, 2010). As with Ukraine, and later Kyrgyzstan, all visa requirements for EU citizens were removed. This may sound like a trite example of "liberalisation", but it serves as a useful illustration of geopolitical aspiration and alignment. In the case of Kyrgyzstan, indeed, the removal of visa requirements for EU and US citizens in the summer of 2012 was unusually radical, particularly in the context of Central Asia, which is generally characterised by illiberal and awkward (for EU citizens) visa regimes.

With the exception of the Baltic States, Georgia remains perhaps the pre-eminent example of a pro-Western, post-Soviet State. However, Kostanyan and Tsertsvadze (2012) argue that, a decade after the Rose Revolution, Georgia remains characterised by an over-reliance on political personalities, as opposed to democratic institutions and "the personality (Saakashvili) credited with leading Georgia to the path of democracy may end up undermining the very process he once started". This, they argue, is largely because the authorities have not encouraged political pluralism, with the major TV companies controlled by the ruling party and "clearly manipulated for political ends". In this context, the "relatively free" virtual space, including blogs and social networks, forms an increasingly critical check on the ruling regime's power.

Georgia's geopolitical significance was illustrated by the attention paid to October 2012's election by Western observers, with it gaining significant and often primetime coverage on the BBC, CNN and other international news agencies and newspapers. Bidzina Ivanishvili's "Georgian Dream" coalition won an unexpected victory, defeating Mikheil Saakashvili in the country's first peaceful post-Soviet transfer of power. Despite the long-standing criticisms outlined here, Saakashvili's legacy is generally positive, partially illustrated by the democratic process that removed him, but unemployment and rates of poverty in Georgia remain high, and many vocal critics remain. Importantly, the constitutional amendments promised by Ivanishvili will not take effect for another year: and Saakashvili remains in office under Georgia's Presidential Republic system.

Key to Ivanishvili's politics is a thawing of relations with Russia. It seems likely that Georgian foreign policy will now begin to more closely resemble that of Armenia, balancing bids to join NATO and support for the EU and US with efforts to revive trade with Russia, which were massively compromised by the war over South Ossetia in 2008 and resultant trade sanctions. Indeed, the 2008 South Ossetian war is likely to remain Saakashvili's most uncomfortable legacy. The breakaway region initially declared independence from Georgia in 1990: this was followed by three smaller conflicts between Georgian forces and those controlling South Ossetia, before escalating into the 2008 war, after which Russian and Ossetian forces gained control of the region. Russia, along with four other countries, now recognises South Ossetia as an independent state, but for most of the international community it remains a *de jure* part of Georgia. A similar situation exists in Abkhazia in North-West Georgia, which is another breakaway region outside the control of the Georgian state. The origins of the 2008 South Ossetia conflict remain disputed, but the majority of international observers summarise it as having been launched by Saakashvili's Georgia shelling the South Ossetian capital of Tskhinvali: an action that was followed by a disproportionate Russian military response. Geopolitical strategy was certainly an additional factor, with Saakashvili gambling on the support of the West to reinforce his overarching pro-US/EU focus, alongside a desire to exploit nationalist domestic sentiment. Many of the journalists interviewed for this book believe that he misjudged his strategy on both counts. Certainly, relations with Russia remained important context behind voting patterns and political strategy during the 2012 elections.

The news media played a crucial role in the electoral process, with one decisive factor being the release of videos of abuse in a large Georgian prison. *The Economist* (2012a) suggested that "although their provenance was unclear, for many the footage crystallised resentment against the arrogance and impunity of Saakashvili's rule". However, the paper added that "by admitting defeat, Mr Saakashvili handed his country a victory and wrong-footed Mr

Ivanishvili, who had said that he would never be allowed to win elections". Many other commentators found cause for optimism in this democratic process, citing how unusual such peaceful transitions are in the post-Soviet world. However, notes of caution frequently accompanied these analyses: with particular mention being made of the dangers inherent in a desire to "right the wrongs" of the Saakashvili regime by, for instance, revisiting past criminal cases with reference to infringed human rights or abuses of power, and thereby initiating a dangerous cycle of retribution (Kumkova, 2012, McLaughlin 2012).

Ukraine

Ukraine's Orange Revolution of 2004 was hailed by many within the country, and particularly in the West, as a decisive break with the past. The events generated a huge amount of international attention, and the prognosis was that the years of "virtual democracy" had been left behind, replaced by an opportunity that would lead the country towards liberal democracy, prosperity and integration into the Euro-Atlantic alliances (Copsey, 2010). However, even at the time there was much scepticism, not least from a significant part of Ukrainian society, broadly located in the Russian-speaking East of the country, that did not support the aims of the Orange Revolution and claimed that the revolution was orchestrated by the US and EU. For Reid (1998), Ukraine exhibits a tenuous, equivocal sense of identity and this cultural and political East/West split remains crucial context behind much Ukrainian political debate.

Similarities with Georgia were discernible throughout the events of the Revolution and their aftermath, although those similarities were rarely highlighted internationally.

Figure 2. Maidan Square in Kiev, Ukraine.

Like Georgia, the protests revolved around dissatisfaction with post-Soviet democratic progress. And, like Georgia, O'Beachain and Polese (2010) argue that the crucial factor in the Orange Revolution was the transformation of informal social networks into formalised civil society groups and NGOs that then mobilised popular support and public protest. So, whereas Ukraine has obvious similarities with Russia and Belarus in terms of its internal cultural identity and historical development, its recent political trajectory and in particular the role of the media and civil society in the run-up to the Colour Revolutions has clear parallels with Georgia. Indeed, the Orange Revolution was even more closely associated with issues of media freedom, as the murder of prominent journalist Georgiy Gongadze (who was of Georgian origin) in 2000 remained a key focal point for the protests against the then President Leonid Kuchma. Gongadze had founded the *Ukrainska Pravda* website, discussed at length in the evidential chapters of this book, a few months before his death in an explicit attempt to circumvent government control over the media.

The millions of protestors involved in the Orange Revolution were also seeking a more general improvement in transparency and living standards, and their demands were subsequently difficult for the newly incumbent politicians to meet. As with the Saakashvili regime in Georgia, the post-revolution presidency of Victor Yushchenko enjoyed only a brief honeymoon period: "The weight of public expectations vested in the Yushchenko presidency in 2005 was so great that it is scant surprise that his administration proved a great disappointment. The Orange 'Revolution' essentially replaced one part of the Ukrainian post-Soviet elite with another" (Copsey, 2010). Indeed, Victor Yanokovych, defeated by the Orange Revolution after attempting to rig elections, returned to power in 2010: an event that many commentators both within and outside Ukraine have connected to increased harassment of independent media, intimidation of political opponents and the manipulation of election laws (Burrett, 2012).

The election campaign of 2005, and many events in Ukrainian politics since then, are often interpreted in both the West and Russia in foreign policy terms: broadly, whether Ukraine leans towards Russia or the EU/NATO. This is further characterised as an electoral, cultural and linguistic divide between a Russian-speaking East exemplified by industrial cities like Donetsk, and a Ukrainian-speaking, Europe-facing West exemplified by Lviv. In fact, however, many of the participants interviewed for this work argued that this characterisation is unhelpfully reductive, and masks the fact that politics in Ukraine, as elsewhere, is generally concerned with more fundamental economic issues and often localised in tone.

By 2012, however, this simplistic cultural geography was being pursued as vigorously as ever by the Western press in the run-up to the European football championships jointly hosted by Ukraine and Poland, albeit in conjunction with more substantive critiques of an increasing tendency towards authoritarianism in the country. President Yanukovych's "counterproductive" persecution of former Ukrainian Prime Minister Yulia Tymoshenko (jailed by the Yanukovych regime in 2011) was repeatedly highlighted by the Western European press. *The Economist* (2012b) argued that Yanokovych's approach to politics is increasingly similar to the autocratic Belarus leader Alyaksandr Lukashenka, and reflects the political culture of the Russian-speaking Donbass region around Donetsk in Eastern Ukraine, which provides him with his powerbase. It conceded, however, that the Ukrainian press remains "vibrant", despite Yanokovych's "bullying" of the media.

Accusations of Yanukovych's illiberal "bullying" also characterised coverage of the run-up to Ukraine's October 2012 Presidential elections, with the UK's *New Internationalist* arguing that the President has "undone many of the Orange Revolution's democratic gains" since regaining office (legally) in 2010 (Burrett, 2012). One of the key "symptoms" of the regime's authoritarian tendencies has been the bullying of journalists, with the pressure group Reporters Without Borders reporting that "independent media are subject to all kinds of harassment, including constant intimidation, raids and prosecutions" (Burrett, 2012). Ukraine is, therefore, arguably the post-Colour Revolution nation to most closely support Hale's thesis that the Colour Revolutions were about cyclical rather than transformational change (Hale, 2005).

Armenia

Armenia receives considerably less international attention than either Ukraine or Georgia. Indeed, such is the geopolitical importance of Kyrgyzstan that it too generates more attention in the West than Armenia. Similarly, Armenia was largely overlooked in the analytical literature on the Colour Revolutions, partly because most political analysts argue that it never had one, in the sense that it never experienced a change of government through peaceful mass protests (Zolyan, 2010). However, it could be argued that the country acted as an archetype for later developments in Ukraine and Georgia, after a disputed election was followed by mass protests and the attempted overthrow of the government in September 1996. The nature of these protests represented an early model for the sorts of peaceful demonstrations that later characterised many post-Soviet environments. Indeed, another specifically Armenian attempt to remove government via peaceful mass protests happened after Georgia's Rose Revolution in Spring 2004, but the establishment managed to retain power.

Since then, Zolyan (2010) argues that Armenia has "imitated democracy" in the sense that formally democratic institutions exist and civil rights are respected, but important resources which could be used by the opponents of the ruling elite to challenge them are controlled by the elite themselves. Relatively tight controls over the media, especially TV, have characterised the post-2004 era: TV stations which could be state run or private are typically controlled by businesses close to the ruling elite, while mainstream print newspapers have seen their circulation collapse.

Figure 3. Republic Square in Yerevan, Armenia.

Armenia has tended to be characterised in recent years by a semi-autocratic elite leading a strong state, but with weaker institutions (associated with higher levels of corruption) than Georgia. Gallina (2010) calls it a "rather bleak picture" in terms of prospects for socio-economic development, despite the fact that the fragmentation between the nationalist and post-Communist elite in both countries has long since ceased.

There have been a number of positive developments in Armenia over the past two years, covered extensively by the interviews later in this book. However, problems remain, characterised by a tendency to solve transitions of power through elite consensus, which is then "legitimised" via elections. This creates an unstable system with a vicious circle in which elite decision-making combines with lack of public participation to decrease confidence in the government (Zolyan, 2010). The country has a recent history of disputed elections, public protests and other crises which are often solved with force, although the General Election of May 2012 passed off without major incident and ended in a largely predictable victory for President Serzh Sargsyan's Republican Party, with Western observers suggesting "ballot stuffing and coercion" was scarce, compared with previous elections (*The Economist*, 2012c).

Armenia's geopolitical situation and long-term post-Soviet strategy has contrasted sharply with that of neighbouring Georgia. It takes a considerably more pragmatic approach to relations with Russia, for example, but attempts to balance this with the continued pursuance of an alliance with the EU. It describes this tactic as a "complimentary foreign policy", which essentially avoids picking sides. The Armenian diaspora helps it achieve this, with one of the world's largest and most significant diasporas (particularly numerous in the US, France and Russia) often funding the wider media within the country. The diaspora has a clear vested interest, both in economic and ideological terms, in avoiding a potentially divisive geopolitical strategy.

The 1990s conflict with neighbouring Azerbaijan over the disputed (ethnically Armenian, geographically Azeri) enclave of Nagorno-Karabakh remains critical relevant context in Armenian politics and media strategy, as does the historically difficult relationship with Turkey. The border with Turkey remains closed, for example, although there have been numerous recent attempts to establish and improve diplomatic ties. Armenia tries to solve its various security dilemmas by cooperating with Russia, again in direct contrast with Georgia. Since 1992, there have been Russian military bases in Armenia close to the Turkish (and therefore NATO) border. In addition, Russian companies continue to dominate certain economic sectors within Armenia. The geopolitics of the region is further complicated by Azerbaijan's oil wealth, which lends it external influence and insulates it from some human rights criticisms, alongside the fact that both Azerbaijan and Armenia border Iran and are therefore of strategic importance to the US as well as Russia.

The mass Armenian protests of April 2004, which followed Georgia's Rose Revolution, attracted little global attention, largely because the opposition failed in its attempts to replicate Georgia's revolution. Observers suggest that the opposition was too weak and lacked a clear programme for development, and several of those interviewed for this book argued that it even lacked a clear political orientation. The populist rhetoric of the opposition stressed nostalgia for the Soviet era and attracted votes among the poor and old, but unsurprisingly failed to win the support of potentially active revolutionary groups like students and young professionals – that is, precisely the demographic that drove the Colour Revolutions in Georgia and Ukraine. The Russian context is significant here too, with Russia fearing a "domino effect" among its potential strategic partners and the Armenian government keen to maintain good relations.

If Ukraine and Georgia have certain similarities post-Colour Revolution, Georgia and Armenia also have some contextual similarities in terms of post-Soviet development. Aside from their geographical proximity as South Caucasian neighbours, Gallina (2010) argues that state structures in both countries still fail to function "for the public's well-being". Further, unresolved territorial issues still characterise political debate in both countries, although the nature of the geopolitical challenges faced by the two differs considerably. Georgia's two breakaway regions are both clearly separatist and distinctive ethnically and linguistically, with both dependent on Russian support. However, Nagorno-Karabakh is essentially a self-governing but ethnically Armenian enclave that is *de jure* within the borders of neighbouring Azerbaijan: therefore its role in Armenian politics, economic development and national identity is very different. Although the conflict over Nagorno-Karabakh ended in 1994, the peace process has stalled and more than sixty people have been killed in skirmishes near the ceasefire line since 2010 (*The Economist*, 2012d).

In August 2012 relations with Azerbaijan worsened considerably following the release of Azeri military officer Ramil Safarov from a Hungarian Prison. Safarov was convicted of killing an Armenian fellow-student during a NATO course for non-member countries in Budapest in 2004. He claimed to be avenging Azeri suffering in the Nagorno-Karabakh conflict, and was hailed as a national hero on his return to Baku. The Armenian government responded by cutting diplomatic relations with Hungary (Tisdall, 2012).

Agitation for change within Armenia continued after the May 2012 election victory of Sargsyan's Republican Party, with Georgia's democratic transfer of power after the October 2012 Georgian Parliamentary election frequently cited. Opposition forces in Armenia cited Saakashvili's defeat as a model for political change in their own country, with Saakashvili lauded for "creating a country where the opposition can win". Notably, however, Armenian

President Sargsyan did not congratulate Ivanishvili on his win (Abbasov and Grigoryan, 2012)

Kyrgyzstan

In an interview with the *Daily Telegraph* in June 2012, former Kyrgyz President Roza Otunbayeva claimed that the overthrow of President Kurmanbek Bakiyev in April 2010 acted as the "spark" for the Arab Spring that began in Tunisia later that year (Kilner, 2012). Otunbayeva became President following the events of April 2010, before standing down in December 2011. Her claim, which seems rather extravagant at first glance, revolves around the fact

Figure 4. Soviet monument in Bishkek, Kyrgyzstan.

that global broadcaster Al Jazeera covered the 2010 Kyrgyz protests in some detail, and that the protestors' demands echoed later movements in the Arab world by targeting corruption and lack of opportunities for the young.

During Otunbayeva's short presidency, a referendum in Kyrgyzstan resulted in a major constitutional change, with power shifted from President to Parliament. The transfer of power led some Western commentators to dub the country Central Asia's first Parliamentary democracy (Kilner, 2012). But, although Otunbayeva claims that the events of 2010 showed that street politics could effectively deal with corrupt and unpopular leaders, Kyrgyzstan remains unstable. It is certainly true that the country is unusually "liberal" when compared to its Central Asian neighbours (who include notoriously repressive long-term autocratic regimes like Uzbekistan and Turkmenistan) and it is this fact, alongside a related set of international alliances that – like Armenia – aims for a pragmatic but rather tenuous balance between Russia and the West, that allows Kyrgyzstan to "punch above its weight" in terms of international attention. However, the flip side to this "beacon of democracy" reputation is a very turbulent recent history and continuing political instability.

That turbulent recent history began with the break-up of the Soviet Union in 1991 and reached an initial climax with the Tulip Revolution of 2005, which enhanced Kyrgyzstan's reputation as a country with an appetite for democracy (and protest) in the heart of an authoritarian "region". Indeed, the country developed a reputation for relative liberalism several years before the Tulip Revolution, with Anderson (1999) dubbing it an "island of democracy". Askar Akaev had been President since the country became independent in 1991. Under Akaev (who, unusually, was an academic rather than a former Soviet apparatchik) Kyrgyzstan began its journey towards a form of "liberalism", with a developed and lively civic society informed by an independent and vibrant media. However, accusations of vote rigging during the 2005 Parliamentary elections, which came in the immediate aftermath of Georgia's Rose Revolution (2003) and Ukraine's Orange Revolution (2004), led to widespread protests. The underlying causes were arguably similar, although the cultural and economic contexts were very different – with Kyrgyzstan a poverty-stricken, non-industrial nation at the margins of the former Soviet Union. As in Ukraine and Georgia, some argued that the events were largely orchestrated by the US, although others argue that the Tulip Revolution was actually deeply rooted in Kyrgyz domestic politics and reflected widespread discontent, not just with the political elite but also in wider society (Lewis, 2010).

Prior to the Tulip Revolution, and during it, the Kyrgyz opposition was considerably less unified than their Georgian and Ukrainian counterparts. A partial result of this lack of focus meant that protests were more spontaneous, and sometimes violent, in tone. In the South of the country, particularly in the cities of Osh and Jalalabad, numerous casualties were recorded. In the capital Bishkek, widespread looting followed the eventual resignation of President Akaev (who by then had fled to Moscow). Akaev would have been the first Central Asian President to voluntarily leave office, and there is some evidence that he had in fact intended to do this (Pannier, 2009).

New Presidential elections were held in July 2005, with Kurmanbek Bakiev gaining power in the first Central Asian election considered by the Organization for Security and

Co-operation in Europe (OSCE) to have been generally free and fair. However, the optimism that greeted his appointment was short-lived and the post-Colour Revolution history of Kyrgyzstan has been considerably more turbulent than that of either Ukraine or Georgia.

Bakiev exhibited an early tendency to crack down on the media, in particular, and threatened several of the freedoms gained under the previous regime. Manzella and Yacher (2005) described the country's media as undergoing an important transitional phase at this time, the central stage of a journalistic rite of passage. The situation worsened, a number of independent journalists were attacked in 2009 (Pannier, 2009) and a degree of nepotism began to characterise Bakiev's political appointments. Thousands of people demonstrated in Bishkek against the Bakiev regime as early as 2006, and again in 2007, although he was re-elected in the 2009 Presidential elections. Unlike the 2005 elections, the OSCE did not come to a positive conclusion about the conduct of the election, suggesting that media bias and ballot fixing were prevalent throughout.

By April 2010, opposition groups had become more organised and protests were escalated. An opposition figure was arrested in the town of Talas on 6 April, providing a catalyst to a further escalation of protests. On 7 April, violent riots and armed clashes between opposition forces and the authorities in Bishkek and elsewhere resulted in the deaths of seventy-six protestors, with Bakiev eventually fleeing the country after being granted asylum by the authoritarian Belarus President Lukashenko. These protests (now often dubbed the "Second Kyrgyz Revolution") attracted the attention of the global media, involving as they did very visible and sustained violence with hundreds of casualties on both sides, and the storming of government buildings. It is now thought that 2000 people died in the subsequent violence in the country as a whole, many in further inter-ethnic rioting that took place in the mixed South of Kyrgyzstan during the power vacuum.

A new interim government was formed under Roza Otunbayeva, which quickly organised the referendum detailed above, which reduced Presidential powers in favour of Parliament: elections were held in October 2010, resulting in a five-way coalition. A degree of instability continues to characterise Kyrgyz politics, however, and this is crucial context for any reading of the immersive interviews later in this book. In August 2012, opposition factions initiated a break-up of the majority coalition, with a new Prime Minister and Government quickly appointed under President Almazbek Atambayev, who won the Presidential election after Otunbayeva voluntarily stepped down in December 2012 (Lee, 2012). This is considered to be Central Asia's first peaceful transition of power following the region's first "genuinely free" elections (Kilner, 2012) [the second, if you accept the OSCE's assessment of the 2005 Kyrgyz election].

It remains the most liberal country in Central Asia, and has continued to undertake reforms that underline this status. For example, visa requirements for most EU countries were dropped in July 2012. It is hard to overstate how unusual this is for the Central Asian region, and it stands as a good illustration of Kyrgyzstan's overarching geopolitical attitudes. More significantly for this book, the coalition government introduced legislation to dispense with all libel laws in 2012. This decision stands as another useful marker for the government's intentions and again reflects the country's unusual ideology. However, its pro-Western leanings are – as in Armenia – balanced with a desire to maintain good relations with Russia. In Kyrgyzstan, this balancing act is arguably even more acute than in Armenia, largely due to the presence of the Manas Air base (now officially known as the Transit Center at Manas), a giant US military installation established in 2001 as a support base for military operations in Afghanistan. President Bakiyev announced in 2009 that the base would be closed, citing public opinion within Kyrgyzstan. However, the announcement followed news of a large package of financial assistance and loans from the Russian government. Later that year, the US dramatically increased its payment for use of the facilities and the base remains open. Currently, all leading political figures in Kyrgyzstan are committed to closing the base in 2014, when the lease runs out. The Kyrgyz government continues to play a difficult geopolitical game, and hosted Russian President Putin in September 2012. The two parties agreed a range of inter-governmental agreements – including extending Russian military bases and the writing off of hundreds of millions of dollars of debt – to the point that many observers argued that there is now a danger of overdependence on Russia in the future (Mashrab, 2012).

Kyrgyzstan retains good relations with Russia, and around 9% of its population classify themselves as ethnic Russians. This figure is significantly lower than during the Soviet era, and ethnic Russians continue to leave the country. As in many former Soviet countries, Russian remains an official language in Kyrgyzstan, and it is still the language of choice in Bishkek. Outside the capital, however, Kyrgyz (a Turkic language) often predominates, and it – again in common with many other former Soviet countries – has increased in political significance since independence, with all leading political posts now requiring fluency in Kyrgyz (which precludes many ethnic Russians and even urban Kyrgyz from occupying those positions).

There is a significant North/South cultural split in Kyrgyzstan. Around 69% of the 5.2 million population are ethnically Kyrgyz, with significant numbers of Uzbeks (15%) concentrated in the South of the country. Ethnic Russians have migrated out of Kyrgyzstan in large numbers since independence, but they still represent 9% of the population, concentrated around Bishkek and other parts of Northern Kyrgyzstan. Smaller numbers of Dungans, Uyghurs and Tajiks represent the largest of the remaining 80 ethnic groups distributed throughout the country. This mosaic reaches its apotheosis in the South of the country, where numerous Uzbek and Tajik enclaves complicate the demographic and political picture. Indeed, the South of the country – around the Fergana valley and the city of Osh – remains a flashpoint for inter-ethnic violence. Hundreds of people were killed in Kyrgyz–Uzbek clashes in Osh in 2010, with the violence escalating to the point that a civil war was feared: 400,000 people were eventually displaced from their homes in the Fergana valley (Recknagel, 2010). However, this 2010 outbreak was the latest in a series of ethnic clashes to have occurred in the South of Kyrgyzstan. As in Georgia and Armenia, the multi-ethnic and multi-lingual nature of Kyrgyzstan is critical context behind any reading of media freedom and journalistic attitudes. Indeed, several of the Kyrgyz correspondents cited reportage from the Osh violence as symptomatic of deeper problems within the Kyrgyz media, notwithstanding its reputation for media freedom and liberalism. In particular, numerous participants cited limitations on the Uzbek population's freedom of expression, arguing that this is particularly noticeable in terms of mainstream journalism. The owners of three Uzbek-language TV stations and two Uzbek-language newspapers all fled Kyrgyzstan following the 2010 Osh violence: and accusations of Kyrgyz repression of the Uzbek media continued to reverberate long after the events. However, even here there are grounds for optimism, with weekly Uzbek newspapers re-established, a new radio station, and, notably, a donor-funded website publishing news in Uzbek (Kumkova, 2012).

Kyrgyzstan's reputation for relative liberalism is rather eclipsed by its poverty. Its democratic credentials have a tendency to be eclipsed by the more urgent demands of the population: such a combination makes political instability almost inevitable. A regional news agency reported that Kyrgyzstan stood on the brink of bankruptcy and economic default in September 2012, as it is running a budget deficit of more than 30% for the second consecutive year since the violent overthrow of President Bakiev.

Media freedom
Ukraine and Georgia's media system is classified as "partly free" by global media watchdog Freedom House, with Armenia and Kyrgyzstan assessed as "not free". The internet is assessed as "free" in all except Kyrgyzstan, where it is "partly free". It should be noted at the outset that, although frequently cited, this organisation is US-based and is regarded as politicised by some analysts, particularly outside the "West": indeed, three interviewees independently cited the Freedom House Press Freedom "score" as an inaccurate reflection of their country's progress, or lack of it. However, the contextual similarities between Georgia and Ukraine is illustrated by Georgia's score of 52 and Ukraine's score of 59 in 2012, although that represents

a considerable shift downwards for Ukraine and upwards for Georgia, as they were within a point of each other in 2011. Equally, the contextual similarities between Armenia and Kyrgyzstan are illustrated by their scores of 65 and 69 respectively (for comparison: Kyrgyzstan's immediate neighbour Uzbekistan recorded one of the worst scores in the world: 95, Iran 92, Kazakhstan 81, UK 21, US 18, Sweden 10). The scores are intended to reflect legal and political pressures on the media as well as economic factors constraining media freedom around the world. Ukraine in particular experienced a "significant decline" in press freedom in 2010, then again in 2011, and an international delegation of press freedom organisations expressed concerns about media and internet freedom in Ukraine in April 2012 (Freedom House, 2012). More serious accusations followed, with the same organisation suggesting that "negative developments" in Ukraine are "at the forefront of an antidemocratic trend in Central and Eastern Europe". Specifically, it argues that Ukraine has suffered significant decline from its Orange Revolution democratic "opening" in an alarmingly short period of time under the Yanukovych government. The economic vulnerability of media outlets, cited by almost all the journalists interviewed in this book as a major barrier to a free press, was pinpointed by the organisation as one of the key issues raising concern about the depth and durability of democracy (Freedom House, 2012).

Ukraine's worsening record on media freedom was also highlighted by the French *Reporters sans Frontieres* organisation, which also monitors freedom of information but uses a different set of criteria to draw up its global rankings. In 2011–12, it ranked Ukraine 116th in global terms, with Kyrgyzstan rising to 108th and Georgia at 104th.

However, it is considerably more optimistic about Armenian media freedom, placing the country 77th globally. For comparison, it placed the post-Soviet Central Asian dictatorship Turkmenistan 177th and Finland/Norway joint first (Reporters Without Borders, 2012). Despite the different approaches of the two organisations, and the fact that all such indices are bound to be regarded as politicised, the contextual similarities between the post-Colour Revolution nations is clear. Reporters Without Borders' 2012 summary concludes by re-stressing its founding principles: that media independence can only be maintained in strong democracies and that democracy needs media freedom (Reporters Without Borders, 2012).

CHAPTER 5

METHOD: THE CHALLENGES OF CROSS-NATIONAL COMPARATIVE MEDIA RESEARCH

The author travelled to Tbilisi (Georgia) in April 2011, Kiev/Kharkov (Ukraine) in February 2012, Yerevan (Armenia) in March 2012, and Bishkek (Kyrgyzstan) in September 2012. The intention was to interview a representative group of journalists about these themes in order to undertake a comparative study of the four countries by analysing the views of those actively involved in online journalism in all four environments. The underpinning motivation was to provide a comparative "snapshot" of the contemporary situation, the rationale being that the wider political situation in all four is rapidly evolving, paralleling the speed with which media technology itself is evolving. The resultant interface between the wider political context and the development and influence of online forms of journalism underpins the study: which seeks to explore the implications via the insights of those involved, and thereby to assess the potential of online journalism through the overarching prism of public interest (Fielden, 2012). Controls on the press are so varied and complex in the former Soviet Union that it is difficult, if not impossible, to meaningfully compare press freedom in one nation with that in another in a purely statistical sense. In one country, newspapers may be under harsh, arbitrary political restraints; in another, they may be under more subtle economic and corporate restrictions (Hachten and Scotton, 2011:26). The attempts by US-based Freedom House to apply an index of Press Freedom illustrate this difficulty: the index, although useful as one of the few attempts to statistically define comparative "media free-dom", was seen as arbitrary and politicised by several of the participants in this study.

Hanitzsch (2008) expresses surprise that comparative methodology is little discussed within the broad area of journalism studies, despite the rising significance of cross-cultural research. He suggests that a tight definition is important and proposes that comparative research should be defined as follows: if two or more a priori defined cultural populations are compared according to at least one functionally equivalent concept. The value of such research derives from its ability to establish the generalisability of theories and also, although this is sometimes less immediately obvious, the validity of interpretations derived from single nation studies.

The problems inherent in this kind of comparative work are numerous, and include the fact that the extent of differences may overwhelm meaningful comparison, and what we treat as a similarity at one level of analysis may reveal myriad differences at more detailed levels of analysis. Qualitative research derived from multiple interviews in multiple contexts inevitably chimes with the old maxim to reveal the complexity without rendering things more opaque (Frake, 1977). However, despite these difficulties, this study argues that a comparative approach is essential if one is to analyse how approaches to online political journalism are evolving in the post-Soviet environment and, if this is to have any validity, it would seem necessary to break free of the problems inherent in a statistical comparative approach (such as that taken by Freedom House and Reporters Without Borders) by aiming instead for a richer contextual comparison based on the more nuanced views of journalists themselves. Livingstone

(2003) makes the case for naturalistic inquiry and qualitative research as a means of accessing people's worlds of meaning in cross-national comparative media research. Such an approach breaks free of the "flat mono-chromatic picture" sometimes associated with statistical approaches and allows for a balance to be struck between rigour and practicality (Archetti, 2012). Theoretical frameworks and concepts can only take analysis so far in this context: there is also a need to know what interventions are happening and how they are working. There is, in short, a need for analyses of practice as well as theory when examining the role of new media in contemporary politics: a need to include the voices of activists and practising journalists to augment scholarly theory (Boler, 2008). Markham (2010) suggests that it should be possible, methodologically, to measure the cultural purchase of particular forms of online journalism: arguing that this should be done not by aggregating page impressions but through qualitative analysis.

For this comparative work to have any validity in the context of practising "voices", it was deemed vital to ensure that all three countries judged to have undergone a "Colour Revolution" were included in the study. Comparative perspectives in this context were intended to secure fresh insights into the factors shaping the emergence and evolution of citizen journalism as a phenomenon in its own right (Allan and Thorsen, 2009). In terms of the broader, independent "hub" websites examined here, comparative perspectives are arguably still more necessary: as the wider geopolitical context is often critical for the development, efficacy and role of online journalism in its broadest and most influential sense. Kyrgyzstan, in particular, presented some logistical problems for the UK-based author, but fieldwork was eventually carried out in all three post-Colour Revolution environments, plus Armenia, and a genuinely comparative analytical and interpretative approach to the overarching topic became possible. The original intention was to supplement the data obtained via the interviews with an attempt to apply Messner and DiStasto's US-centric "source cycle" theory (2008) to the post-Soviet context, by statistically assessing the sourcing relationship between online journalism and the mainstream press. However, the linguistic barriers inherent in a true assessment of this relationship in five languages made this unfeasible: any assessment would have been tokenistic in this context. More importantly, the interviews revealed that online journalism in the post-Soviet environments examined here is sidestepping the mainstream press entirely: with a US-style "source cycle" notable largely by its absence.

Hanitzsch et al.'s large-scale comparative study of journalist's attitudes (2011) followed Hofstede's (2001) alternative method by constructing "matched samples" that allow for comparison across countries because of their similar compositions. The volume of material processed by Hanitzsch et al.'s study (2011), and the number of countries involved in the comparison, necessitated such an approach. By contrast, the comparative study in question was deliberately restricted to four countries and involved a series of immersive, semi-structured interviews with journalists: all of whom were active political (print) journalists, and all of whom had some knowledge and experience of online journalism within the context of the countries in question. This latter requirement was intended to parallel Hanitzsch et al.'s "matched samples", albeit on a smaller scale, by ensuring the sample group was as coherent as possible to allow for a meaningful comparison across countries in terms of perspective and policy.

The selection process was therefore multi-faceted. In the first instance, a group of journalists from a range of Georgian independent news websites and conventional newspapers were interviewed during an initial research visit to Tbilisi, Georgia. This panel interview formed the basis for the immersive individual interviews which followed, with questions revolving around the political role and efficacy of independent websites in Georgia. The emergence of one or two particularly influential "hub" websites was noted during this first panel discussion. However, the author sought to retain a neutral position on the topic, not least because the question of which "hub" website was most influential depends largely on users' interpretations of political influence and cannot be meaningfully "predicted" via usage statistics. Subsequently, the author sought to arrange interviews with journalists involved in the writing of online news in Ukraine, Armenia and Kyrgyzstan.

Collated sources of global online journalism were consulted alongside web traffic sites indicating online news agencies with the largest number of site visits in order to approach relevant journalists to request an interview: Global Voices, an international online community that reports on citizen media, was found to be particularly useful in this respect. Such collated sources provided a basis for participant selection, alongside direct approaches to the leading online news agencies (by web traffic statistics) in each environment.

It is important to note that all journalists interviewed had some practical experience of writing for an online audience, even if their "day job" was on a conventional print newspaper. This requirement was made clear in the emailed request for interview. For the purposes of the study, journalists were further defined as those who had some level of editorial (writing) responsibility. Within these criteria, an attempt was made to select participants according to editorial team hierarchy and, subsequently, willingness to participate (editors were approached first, followed by deputies, followed by chief reporters). The size of the sample was compromised somewhat by time and resources: none of the locations was visited for longer than a week. However, an attempt was made to standardise the sample size by approaching between fifteen and twenty journalists in each country, all conforming to the requirements outlined above. In the event, interviews were conducted with between seven and nine journalists in all four countries, and the specifics of this are further outlined below.

In terms of the interviews themselves, a series of basic research tools were developed in advance of the interviews to ensure intercultural validity, and to ensure that the comparative approach could be meaningfully explored by merging the evidential content from the interviews in all three countries. The intention was to develop an outline conceptualisation of the fundamental issues addressing both the deficiencies of conventional journalism and the related potential for online journalism in order to formulate four simply worded, leading questions for discussion that could be meaningfully applied in three distinctive national contexts. The simple wording was deliberate and necessary for comparative purposes, and this semi-structured approach was intended, in particular, to allow *participants* to define the role of online media within their respective journalistic environments, rather than the researcher.

Underpinning this approach was an intention to obtain a richer, more nuanced and meaningful assessment of the role of online journalism within the two countries. This qualitative approach, based on the perspective of "insiders", seeking a holistic picture of what evolving media technology actually means in these contexts in relation to journalistic ideals and the wider public and political sphere, was further assisted by the author's professional experience as a journalist: which allowed, in some cases, for more open discussion, as the author was able to mobilise and reference a professional perspective on many of the issues under discussion. Galtung (1990) argues for theoretical pluralism in such circumstances: a range of approaches aimed, ultimately, at a richer exploration of that "snapshot" in time.

Hanitzsch (2008) argues that only a few scholars have explained and justified their choice of comparative strategy. Cultures need deliberate selection for meaningful causal relationship (hence the strict focus on post-Colour Revolution environments) and constructs used to define units of analysis must be equivalent across all cultures. An editor's role may vary across cultures for instance. The same set of methods needs to be used, in this case semi-structured interviews, but even the same method of date collection may produce different behaviours among respondents of different cultural and linguistic backgrounds. Questions should have broadly equivalent meaning in all included cultural populations; items intended to measure a particular construct should be designed to ensure valid and equivalence measurement in all studied cultures (Hanitzsch, 2008)

The four deliberately simplified questions were therefore posed to all participants, with subsequent discussion adapted to fit the specificities of each country, particularly when exploring the significance of recent political developments (for instance, the 2011 arrest of former Prime Minister Yulia Tymoshenko in Ukraine, the recent calls for autonomy among the Armenian minority in one region of Georgia, and the imminent [at the time of the interviews] May 2012 General Election in Armenia). Ideally more immersive interviews would have been conducted, but time and resources prevented this. In Tbilisi, circumstances meant that five of the journalists were interviewed as a panel, alongside subsequent immersive interviews with four individual Georgian journalists. In Ukraine, all eight interviews were with individual journalists in separate locations. In Armenia, seven immersive interviews were conducted with individual journalists, all in separate locations. In Kyrgyzstan, eight immersive interviews were conducted, all in separate locations. Some of these interviews took place at the participants' place of work, others took place at "neutral" venues: cafes, restaurants and the like. The meeting places were all arranged in advance of the author's visit: and the author allowed the participants to decide on their preferred venue in an effort to render the interview process as convenient and comfortable as possible.

With the exception of two journalists in Tbilisi, who were interviewed in the company of a translator, all those questioned spoke English. Clearly, this is not ideal as the sample immediately becomes artificially selective. However, the comparative nature of the study, in four distinctive linguistic environments, made it essential. Further, the web-based focus of the study tended to mean that those journalists approached to participate, in both countries, were young (all under 40, with a clear majority under 30) and therefore far more likely to speak English than older journalists trained under the Soviet system (who tend to speak Russian as a second language). Indeed, the tendency to use Russian as a lingua franca is diminishing among young people, particularly in Georgia, hence the need for a comparative study to be conducted in English. Independence has tended to lead to an increased political emphasis on the indigenous language, at the expense of Russian, across the post-Soviet world. Indeed, had the author made an attempt to conduct these interviews in Russian, any pretence at "neutrality" would inevitably have been compromised, as the geopolitical situation renders language inherently political in all four countries.

The post-Soviet context is equally crucial in the professional context: all those interviewed received journalistic training *after* the Soviet era. The perspective of Soviet-trained journalists was frequently cited by participants as a key inhibitor of mainstream journalism in their countries, with many interviewees arguing that online journalism's trusted status was at least partially explained by the fact that the mainstream print press remains dominated by older, Soviet-trained journalists.

Most of the participants in all four countries requested anonymity, and while some allowed their full names to be quoted in the study, it was felt to be more prudent to anonymise all interviewees by using forenames only for identification purposes. This was made clear to all participants before the interviews began. One journalist in Ukraine, and one journalist in Kyrgyzstan, requested full anonymity: this is made clear in the text.

The following research questions were posed to all participants in each country:

1. What are the barriers to conventional journalism?
2. What is the relationship between online news media, the mainstream press and politics?
2b. Are there any genuinely influential online political websites?
3. How are minorities covered in the media?
3b. What role does online journalism have in the portrayal of minority linguistic and ethnic groups?

The intention was for the interviews to follow a logical discursive progression: Question (1) was intended to gain the participants' perspectives on what they saw to be the deficiencies of the mainstream media in their respective countries, and to act as a contextual and discursive lead in to the second question, (2), an open question on the role and impact of online political journalism. A follow-up question on influential websites (2b) was asked only if the participant specifically mentioned a website after question (2), and is absorbed into that section in the analysis below. Finally (3), the coverage of, and representation of minorities within each country was included as a "litmus test" for many related issues of media freedom and democracy. Again, where relevant in the subsequent discussion this was expanded on in a further question (3b), which asked participants to consider the current and potential role of online journalism in the representation and coverage of minority ethnic and linguistic communities, which may otherwise be ignored or misrepresented by the mainstream press. Ahmed (2012) argues that the inability of countries to either incorporate minority groups into a liberal and tolerant society or resolve what he calls the "centre versus periphery" conflict is emblematic of a systemic failure of the modern state.

Evidence from qualitative research across the social sciences suggests that the processes involved in interpreting a question and formulating an answer are complex. For example, if the researcher re-words questions, responses from participants tend to change. If the interviewer provides even slightly amended response options then people will give different answers (Clarke and Schober, 1992). This is an inevitable result of human interaction, although attempts can be made to standardise the process as much as possible and therefore minimise possible bias or variation between the groups, and individual participants. The author made an attempt to standardise the three leading questions, as the immersive nature of individual interviews allowed for this, in order to avoid potential sources of bias that inevitably arise when questions are reworded. This was particularly important in terms of the validity of this study: as questions were posed to individual journalists in four very different cultural environments. Instead, discussion was allowed to progress and evolve after the standardised leading questions with a small amount of country-specific prompting from the author. However, this does not, of course, lead to standardisation of "meaning" from the perspective of the participants. Instead, understanding is often affected by a range of social and cultural factors, and this is clearly particularly relevant when conducting a comparative study in four countries. As previously stated, the author attempted to overcome some of these issues by ensuring that all participants were drawn from similar journalistic backgrounds.

However, undertaking work that assesses the real impact of online political journalism is unavoidably problematic when working as an individual researcher. Focusing on a single theme and striving for a level of social coherence among the groups helps, but ultimately the validity of studies such as this is inevitably compromised by scale. That said, it is also apparent that immersive interviews lend themselves to more natural conversation and thus produce some interesting, often revealing responses. The overarching aim was to allow the participants to explore the questions naturally and in their own time, in order to gain a contextually rich set of responses.

While inferences and real meaning in this context remain problematic for the researcher, individual interviews allow for in-depth probing and exploration of the meaning the respondent intends to convey with their reply, a crucial part of the interviewing process (Suchman and Jordan, 1992). The author attempted to engage in some prompting of this sort, as this interactional technique to clarify meaning is almost unavoidable during human contact, with the process intended to mimic the process of natural conversation where attempts are usually made to establish the speaker's real intended meaning, or check that their own message has been properly understood. The issue of meaning is obviously central to understanding subjective views like this, hence the vital importance of assessing interviewees' understanding of questions. However, too much prompting would have been inappropriate given the scale and scope of the focus groups. This unobtrusive, relatively minimal approach to prompting was intended to avoid altering the interview dynamic and meant that much of the exploration of the meaning of the responses was conducted during analysis of the data rather than in collaboration with the interviewees.

A degree of prompting is inevitable, however, and can be further rationalised by the fact that participants sometimes have to make suppositions to answer questions. Evidence from cognitive research suggests that many people will respond even if they do not understand the question (Clarke and Schober, 1992), and therefore inconsistencies in response should alert the interviewer to comprehension problems. One of the obvious further weaknesses with this kind of research, first highlighted by the work of Morley (1980), is the reliance on what respondents *choose* to disclose, and, crucially for this study, what they are able to articulate about the democratising potential of online journalism. There is also evidence that people strive to be consistent when they answer questions and might choose logically consistent responses even if this does not reflect their views (Clarke and Schober, 1992).

The interviews stand alone despite the author's initial plan to conduct a content analysis of the key hub websites in each environment. As highlighted earlier in this chapter, this proved impossible to conduct equally in all four contexts, as a meaningful content analysis would have demanded competence in all four languages, along with Russian. An initial attempt was made to assess the relationship between the Georgian *Netgazeti* site and the Georgian mainstream press with a view to applying Messner and DiStasto's (2008) "source cycle" theories to the post-Soviet context, but it was felt that this would ultimately have been tokenistic in the context of the work as a whole, in which a comparative treatment of all four environments was of central importance. Indeed, the decision to analyse the interviews in thematic chapters, rather than analysing the responses from each country in turn, was taken in order to further facilitate a meaningful comparative study. The desire to retain contextual richness whilst lending the study a meaningful framework was the overriding factor behind this decision.

CHAPTER 6

EVIDENTIAL: WHAT ARE THE BARRIERS TO CONVENTIONAL JOURNALISM?

All interviewees in all four countries were initially asked an open-ended, context-setting question about what they see as the main barriers to conventional, mainstream journalism in their respective countries. There was a notable degree of commonality in the immediate responses, with the majority of interviewees focusing on financial constraints and declining circulation, together with issues of objectivity which revolved around what most (but not all) participants described as a degree of "self-censorship". Significantly, journalists in Kyrgyzstan were *least* likely to stress "self-censorship" as a barrier to journalism, despite the fact that the country's "media freedom" rating is the lowest of the four analysed (Freedom House, 2012). The Georgian respondents also stressed criticisms of recent government actions towards the news media, emphasising what they saw as the damage caused by political developments in the period before the General Election of October 2012. Responses are sometimes merged in order to provide a more meaningful comparison between the four countries: an attempt is made to identify contextual similarities between countries where these are notable and relevant. At times, however, the direction of the discussion inevitably progressed in a country-specific direction: in such cases, the views of several participants from a single country are analysed together within the overarching thematic framework.

Nino R, Georgia: Together with the problem of public information accessibility, the independent press and online media outlets are facing a serious financial crisis in Georgia ... that's the first thing we should say. The most obvious effect of this is that media organisations trying to provide the public with balanced news are often less attractive for advertisers ... who generally steer clear of advertising in the kind of online or print publications that publish investigative articles or offer readers, er, what we might call *critical* analysis of government reforms.

Katerina, Georgia: Things have got a bit worse recently, but actually, the ... signs were there quite early. Changes happened quickly after the Rose Revolution, you know. Just a month after Saakashvili came to power, popular TV stations shut down one after another. The Georgian media just has not been able to play the role expected of it since the Rose Revolution. The best journalists obviously refuse to simply transmit official statements, so they tend to work in the independent media. But this means their work gets a small audience.

Broadcast information is often misleading, unbalanced and partisan in Georgia, with the 2011 Media Sustainability Index report noting that "political bias often comes not in the form of Western-style, value-based leanings, but rather outright propaganda and counter-propaganda". This is despite guarantees for free speech being enshrined in the Georgian constitution immediately after the Rose Revolution in 2004, which provides clear principles to safeguard against the abuse of restrictions on freedom of speech (Yerevan Press Club, 2011).

Nino M, Georgia: It's true enough to say that media legislation in Georgia often seems near-perfect, certainly surprisingly liberal. But media company owners will tell you it all helps the government to implement, um, what we might call ... indirect but obvious pressure on journalists. There is almost no transparency in terms of media ownership and this is a huge problem. Georgians don't know who is delivering the news to them.

Salome, Georgia: Rustavi 2 [TV channel] really just represents the Saakashvili government, with Imedi TV a bit more independent. Saakashvili knows the power of the media, he keeps an eye on the media, there's no question.

Direct censorship has been alleged, and there are also concerns about the representation of minority linguistic and ethnic groups (covered in more depth in Chapter 8). The media, and NGOs in general, were particular targets for the Saakashvili regime, which lost power in the Georgian election of October 2012 (after the interviews took place):

The sometimes coarse methods to accomplish reforms, the weak opposition in Parliament, and the identification of President Saakashvili with an enlightened autocratic leaders such as Kemel Ataturk justify the paradoxical expression that under Shevardnadze, Georgia was a hybrid democracy without democrats, whereas under Saakashvili, Georgia was led by a democratic ideal of image, without being a democracy. (Companjen, 2010, p. 27.)

The Ukrainian response to this first leading question was notably similar, but some participants took the opportunity to relate media deficiency with wider cultural changes in the country. Indeed, with the exception of the Georgian participants, all interviewees briefly discussed the "Soviet context" when addressing the contemporary problems of the conventional print press, in the sense that a culture of newspaper reading still existed as a hangover from Soviet times, but that this had often failed to translate to a robust private newspaper sector.

> Vitaly, Ukraine: Soviet people, if we can call them that, had a culture of reading newspapers, and indeed reading generally. In fact the entire education system, was, I would say, built around people reading papers and books. That culture of reading through traditional media is vanishing. This is partly explained, in my view, by the lack of colour. I, er … think I mean that in two ways. Newspapers in Ukraine are dull, they cover dull topics, and they are *literally* dull … I mean, they're in black and white. Magazines, of the gossip variety, yellow journalism, whatever you want to call it, expanded in the last decade because they were in colour. Again, in both senses … they were lively and colourful. For lots of people, worrying numbers of people, they have replaced news, politics, discussion. You know, only one or two newspapers are now seen in Kiev – and what's very worrying is that there's a big middle to lower income older audience that lacks web access.

Participants in all countries referred to self-censorship as a major and continuing problem, although the Ukrainian journalists were the most likely to stress the issue. It seems possible to speculate that this may relate to the fact that Ukrainian media is more established, more "European" in terms of journalistic conventions, and on a considerably larger scale than that of the three other countries analysed: therefore, there is perhaps a greater sensitivity to issues such as self-censorship.

> Tetyana, Ukraine: There is self-censorship, certainly, we censor ourselves … as journalists, I mean, we censor ourselves. How will what I write be received? It's not like the

days of Kuchma [the second President of independent Ukraine] with direct censorship but rather, still, a question of self-censorship. Let me be clear: self-censorship has definitely gone up since Yanukovych [came to power]. After the Orange Revolution, there was a feeling of freedom, but now this form of censorship has returned. It's not the same as before the Orange Revolution but it's definitely increasing.

One of the interviewees in Kiev took a particularly negative view of the country's journalism and political system: this participant requested full anonymity. Again, he responded to the first question by mentioning self-censorship, but immediately introduced a different take on the issue.

M, Ukraine: You hear a lot of political activists and independent-minded journalists talking about the problems of self-censorship but, look, in my view self-censorship is too soft a term for what goes on here. They do this, censor themselves, because otherwise they'd be fired. It's that simple. I was speaking to a local journalist in Kiev recently who said that everyone, or all the trouble-makers at least, have been fired on his paper ... I'll give you an example of what I mean by this. On my paper we tried to run a particular story that got us into trouble, but the journalists on other papers I spoke to just couldn't understand it. They said: "why didn't you just pull the story?" They just didn't get it. People still want state jobs here – it's the biggest evidence the system just isn't working. Ukrainian journalists come to our paper and say "I can't imagine writing this without being fired". Journalists don't know how to be journalists here, they don't know what a good lead is, they often can't write.

In the media sphere in many post-Communist contexts, the so-called Anglo-American model of journalism has been widely accepted as a norm of professional attitude and quality journalism, even though it is in part a myth (e.g. Hallin and Mancini, 2004), and even though concepts of journalistic performance are strongly influenced by journalistic traditions in different countries (Jakubowitz, 2001). The views of "M" above, chime with this latter viewpoint, with his suggestion that mainstream media deficiencies are systemic and cultural, rather than merely structural or economic, in their origin.

Over a decade ago, Splichal (2001) argued that although the media in post-Socialist states have made significant gains in terms of liberalisation and pluralisation, they "remain vulnerable to manipulation by political forces and, in addition, became dependent on commercial corporations". While countries like Bulgaria and Romania have made considerable progress in this respect, partially necessitated by membership of the EU, the post-Soviet journalistic environment in the former USSR remains compromised by older traditions echoing Soviet practices. It is notable that the views of many of the Ukrainian interviewees echoed McNair's decade-old suggestion that the "Bolshevik psychology" of the post-Soviet media professional lingered in many cases, effectively negating many of the reforms put in place by the new regimes. This centred around a conviction that the role of the journalist is to be an ideological partisan of the politician, party or organisation to whom he or she "belongs". Media outlets take sides then impose a certain editorial position on their employees (McNair, 2001).

M, Ukraine: If you wanted to launch a successful newspaper in Ukraine it would be easy – you'd write about corruption, politicians taking bribes, you know … all that stuff. No politicians have a real vision for the country, they all just want power, and that's the explanation for what I see as the false East/West split conjured up by politicians and the press [this refers to the cultural "divide" between Russian-speaking Eastern Ukraine and Ukrainian-speaking, Europe-facing West, and is covered in more depth in section 3]. There's no positive vision for the country, in other words ... Look, the East/West split is not a problem. What people want is to see people attacking the corrupt but you won't see that in any newspaper because nobody would fund it. *Ukrainska Pravda* is the one paper to do this. It's only online, and it has Danish sponsors I think. These guys are very good, they do proper investigative journalism, you know what I mean. Part of the problem is that there is zero trust of newspapers. Mainstream journalism here is used to taking money for articles. Proper journalism is not mainstream, it's niche, it's online.

Notably, this participant independently raised the online "solution" to deficiencies in the mainstream, without prompting by the author and before the question that was intended to address the issue specifically. Other Ukrainian participants held similar, though somewhat less critical, views on the issue of mainstream journalistic deficiencies.

Tetyana, Ukraine: With Yanokovych [Victor Yanukovych, President since narrowly defeating Tymoshenko in January 2010] all the good progress seemed to go back the other way. If you do an interview, er, you have to send the article over for inspection, and people ... journalists, do this naturally. Also, I should say, the systems of paper distribution are terrible.

Ukraine, Georgia and, to a lesser extent, Armenia and Kyrgyzstan all profess allegiance to "Western" concepts of free press as it relates to democracy, and Ukraine and

Georgia both have EU membership as a long-term policy objective. However, in all these countries there remain tensions with regard to control of the mainstream press. Notably, incidents of censorship and other forms of state control over the news media have increased sharply since the events of the "Arab Spring". Indeed, the idealistic elements of the Arab Spring were echoed (although not necessarily directly linked) by opposition protests in all four countries during 2011. These protests were relatively small scale and generated little global news coverage but many had significant consequences. In Georgia, for example, protests in 2011 relating to media freedom and other issues resulted in the arrests and imprisonment of numerous high-profile journalists (this claim was related independently by three of the Georgian interviewees).

Vitaly, Ukraine: People who are emotionally driven are willing to spend extra time working on stories about politics – this is precisely the reason that independent websites like *Ukrainska Pravda* are thriving, along with some notable blogs. Fewer professional journalists see their, ah, working place as a space for creativity because they're limited by low salaries and what I would call forms of, well, censorship. Political censorship is often mixed up with editorial policy that derives from owners who are often politicians interested in media assets. This is not necessarily the same as direct censorship. I'll give you the example of *Sevodnya*, which is controlled by a Donetsk tycoon, who, er, fired the editor after he carried a ... controversial story and appointed a new manager who was, erm, loyal to the government but a failure professionally. This was a scandal. It's complicated: on the one hand there's growing censorship as shown by this case, on the other hand editors try to follow their investors and not harm their interests.

Other Ukrainian participants stressed more fundamental structural problems, suggesting that the future of the mainstream press was fatally compromised by a combination of technology, global recession, and, perhaps more importantly, a widespread lack of trust in the media. Maksym chose to illustrate this with the same example of malpractice.

> Maksym, Ukraine: Print journalism is dying very fast in Ukraine. Two years ago I would see a lot of people reading newspapers, on the metro, on buses, but two weeks ago I realised I hasn't seen anyone reading a paper for months. Hundreds of small papers in Ukraine are supported by local authorities, and they are struggling with funds. The 2008 recession more or less destroyed the print business in Ukraine. Also, people just don't believe newspapers – the level of journalism ... the, erm ... quality, is low. The popular sites cover everything but they do it in a tabloid style. Here's an example from Sevodnya, owned by the richest man in Ukraine. A journalist wrote an article about the President's house ... soon after that article they had problems and, erm, the editor was fired. So now they avoid news about politicians.

Journalists in Armenia were perhaps the most critical of the traditional media environment, notably print, with all participants beginning their interviews by highlighting the dramatic crash in circulation that followed the initial post-Soviet peak. Two participants partially linked this crash to the recent upsurge in web-based news sites.

> Artur, Armenia: Hardly anyone reads newspapers any more in Armenia. Soviet newspapers used to have a huge audience but they were ... toilet paper really. There was an old Soviet newspaper culture, of course, here in Armenia

as much as in Latvia, Moscow, Kiev ... anywhere else. Then, the new diaspora founded and funded a range of new papers after independence in '91 – some of these quickly rose to 100,000 circulation or even more. Those were pretty free papers, then ... for some reason, people got tired of this freedom.

The Armenian diaspora, one of the largest in the world, remains an important part of the country's political context and was closely associated with the development of a free press in the immediate post-Soviet era. This participant was then asked to clarify his final comment.

Artur, Armenia: Look, what I think is ... er, what *most* of us think is that Armenian journalists have never learned to be competitive. This is why people got tired, the journalism, the standards, just weren't good. By 2005 the same papers [those with a circulation of 100,000+ in the early 1990s] were seeing a print run of 4,000. That is quite a crash, you'd agree. Editors found other ways to get funded instead – mainly, from sponsors in government. Now they don't bother to increase their print run. They don't have the motive to do so: politicians give them cash to stay as they are. Armenian journalists work for specific interests: they are not interested in serving the people.

Omnik, Armenia: The main barrier to mainstream journalism here is the need for self-sustainability and the question of political or economic ownership. These two issues are ... still very much urgent here.

The problem with the Armenian print media, in other words, is structural and systemic, but does not (according to the participants at least) relate to censorship because the low levels of circulation render them essentially irrelevant.

Artur, Armenia: We do have papers that are highly critical of the government. Pretty good freedom, they can do ... whatever they want. But one reason for this, and it's worth stressing, is that this is because *nobody reads them.* The government doesn't monitor them – it doesn't care. If they sold more then they would soon start to get interested.

A similar pattern is identifiable in the recent trajectory of the print press in all four countries. A strong and long-established newspaper reading tradition, deriving from the Soviet era, followed by an initial embrace of a free print press before disenchantment sets in as newspapers fail to capitalise on their early promise. Participants in all four countries referred to the poor standard of journalism in the indigenous print press and, particularly, to what they saw as the tedious content of many newspapers. As a partial result, television news remains considerably more influential in all four countries. This can have major implications in terms of the vibrancy of the public sphere, particularly in the small-scale media environment of Armenia, which retains close ties with Russia and where Russian influence and the Russian media footprint, although waning slightly, remains hugely important.

Sonia, Armenia: We have three Russian TV news channels. Russian public TV is huge here, still. In terms of influence I'm not sure, it's hard to say how influential it is. But, er, it is definitely true that Armenian TV cannot handle this competition. It pales by comparison because obviously Russian TV has far more resources. It's, you know, an unfair situation, it's quite a big issue ... There's an age thing going on here too. Younger people stay away from TV, because they're all online, but older people still watch Russian TV, which takes the advertising revenue as a result. Young people are starting to struggle with Russian [language], and the TV audience has declined a lot because those young people are … staying away, so I really don't know what will happen in 10, 15 years' time.

One participant had a revealing perspective on the recent history of Armenian television news: as with the Ukrainian and Georgian participants, he independently raised online journalism as a form of "solution" to these structural media problems before the interviewer posed a more specific question.

> Gegham, Armenia: I'm a former TV journalist myself, but the A1+ station I worked on was shut down for political reasons. It was shut down but it's now a website. This is where the real influence is now in Armenia. The numbers accessing it may not be high but they're the … er, middle classes, they have … opinions, you know? In terms of conventional newspapers, it's a bad situation. The Armenian Times is the main paper for opposition but it has a circulation of 6,720, it's nothing … peanuts, you know. Its editor was jailed as an opposition leader. Have you seen it? [shows the newspaper]. It's like … a pamphlet, it's eight pages long, black and white, five issues per week, none on Sunday or Monday.

This participant also emphasised the distinctive trajectory of the Armenian press since independence.

> Gegham, Armenia: It's not a new situation. Our print press, you know … after an initial boom, then collapse, collapse, collapse. One of my friends calls our newspapers "letters from the government". But he might have added "or the opposition", because some of them are mouthpieces of the opposition. But that's all they are, that's the word, mouthpieces. The problem is low circulation too. Even in 2008 we were down to around 12,000 on papers

but websites now have 60–100,000 visitors a day. To be honest, websites steal information from printed papers. At 5 am they steal stories, they pick off the best ones.

This form of online plagiarism was also mentioned in Kyrgyzstan and is explored in more detail in the next chapter. Indeed, there were some notable contextual similarities between participants' responses in Armenia and Kyrgyzstan despite the very different cultural and geographical setting, perhaps partly because both are small countries in terms of population, with significant economic and social problems. Kyrgyzstan is arguably the most revealing of the four countries studied and, despite some contextual similarities with the other three countries, participants' perspectives were frequently distinguished by their tendency to relate the issues to the prevailing political situation, which remains in a state of flux. At the time of the visit, in September 2012, for instance, the regime was in the process of responding to a referendum which allowed for the transfer of power from President to Parliament: in the context of Central Asia, this was seen as a highly significant transition towards Parliamentary democracy (*The Economist* 2012d). Kyrgyzstan had also (July 2012) dispensed with all visa requirements for most EU citizens, and, even more notably for this research, dispensed with all media libel laws. It is hard to overstate just how radical such policies are in Central Asia, which has long had a reputation for authoritarianism and illiberality, but these democratic policies did not emerge from a vacuum: the country has a post-Soviet history of intermittent and unusual (for the region) experiments with political openness, relative media freedom and democracy. However, these "experiments" began to coalesce in 2012, two years after the revolution which overthrew President Bakiev in 2010. As a result, most (but not all) Kyrgyz journalists interviewed were buoyant, although pragmatic, about prospects for the news media in their country. This had the perhaps inevitable effect of rendering the responses notably optimistic. Indeed, journalists in Kyrgyzstan were, as a group, the most optimistic respondents to this first leading question.

Aslan, Kyrgyzstan: In Kyrgyzstan right now it's the freest time I can say ... I can remember ... in that way. I worked under President Bakiev, and others, and it's definitely better now. Four presidents I worked under ... and now is the best. I'd say ... I would almost say ... complete freedom. Sometimes it's interesting because I compare it to other countries. Not just regional countries, not just Uzbekistan, Kazakhstan, but – let's say – Asia [as a whole]. Our journalism is in ... the progress, the process of change, it's finding its way, but we can be more, er ... flexible. Our laws are ... not so strict, and this means that newspapers, websites sometimes just ... lift stories, there is some, er, copycat journalism. We're very ... flexible, though, especially compared to Asian countries like Singapore. I studied there for a while and found out that they didn't, er ... write much there. So I was cautious here at first when I came back and was soon criticised for not being tough enough.

There was broad agreement among the Kyrgyz participants about this. The views of Kuban, for instance, chimed with those of Aslan, but he quite quickly introduced a note of caution: specifically linking increased media freedom to an increase in political instability.

Kuban, Kyrgyzstan: Over the last two years the media has become very free in Kyrgyzstan. At the moment the big issue is that they've removed libel from legislation. You can write anything you want. That can sometimes create .... er, problems of its own because Kyrgyz-language papers are ... yellow press, with lots of unconfirmed stuff. You know, they were like that *before* they changed the libel laws ... happy to publish rumours and gossip about, er, public figures, so who knows what they'll be like in a few months' time. There's already lots of scandals involving politicians: they can do nothing ... I think things will be quite unstable over the next two years. By this, I don't necessarily mean ... turmoil ... but I do mean that we'll see frequent political changes and short [lived] regimes. I think that much more activism is likely towards 2015, the next elections, and I think the media will clearly have a role in that. You know, the opposition is already very, er, vocal, very much ... more active and mobilising. It has a voice in the press. And you've also got groups outside Parliament who would like to dissolve it.

The post-Tulip revolution history of Kyrgyzstan has been particularly unstable, as detailed in the overview chapter: indeed, it has arguably been the most unstable country in the former Soviet Union. At the time of the research visit in September 2012, the 2010 violence in Bishkek, which resulted in 2,000 deaths in Kyrgyzstan as a whole, was fresh in many people's minds. Despite the legislative measures taken by the Kyrgyz government, few of those interviewed seemed optimistic about future stability – often linking post-Tulip revolution gains in freedom, media included, to political instability. That said, there was always an acknowledgement that this system, this instability, remained preferable to the authoritarianism of some of its neighbouring countries in Central Asia. In a rapidly evolving political situation, with a country stumbling towards a form of democracy in a region noted for authoritarianism, a degree of instability is perhaps inevitable. Moves towards media freedom and other forms of democratic accountability therefore contribute to political instability, for better or worse. One participant provided an example of the real political effects of this media freedom, while simultaneously questioning the full extent of that freedom, suggesting that quotes and comments were misconstrued and sometimes deliberately misinterpreted by the opposition.

> Begaim, Kyrgyzstan: It is impossible to claim that there is ... a freedom of speech in Kyrgyzstan. It may seem like this, but many mass media are under control of this or that political group who ... put their views across by using that so-called, er, freedom. One MP left government recently because he said that his party was ... in some way, er, involved in the 2010 ethnic clashes [between ethnic Kyrgyz and Uzbeks in the Southern city of Osh and other areas of Southern Kyrgyzstan, including other parts of the notoriously unstable Fergana valley, with a patchwork of ethnic and linguistic loyalties]. This statement in the media led to more clashes, some more violence and ... protests, even though he said he was misquoted by the press.

> Kuban, Kyrgyzstan: The system is predisposed to instability. Even at the moment some groups want elections earlier than 2015, and they're pushing for that to happen. There are always people who want to change the PM and this is mainly for ... political reasons, not economic. Parliament here tends to, ah ... *create* public outrage. Physical violence is quite frequent in Parliament, never mind outside it. The media's relationship to this is complicated. Sometimes they ... add to this outrage, sometimes they calm it.

One journalist took a very different perspective when addressing this first question. Whereas almost all the other Kyrgyz journalists began by stressing the degree of media freedom enjoyed by journalists in the country, and were sometimes even critical of the political effects of that freedom, she retained more fundamental concerns about the standard of journalism in the country, and questioned the real degree of that freedom, in addition to highlighting structural problems faced by the media. As such, her response was closer to that of participants in Ukraine and Georgia. It is, perhaps, relevant to note that this participant was an ethnic Russian born and raised in Kyrgyzstan and, as such, part of a dwindling population of ethnic Russians remaining in the country.

> Elena, Kyrgyzstan: The media here is ... partially free ... maybe. But not fully free ... not at all. Journalists still can't publish articles about corruption. That's the obvious example, the obvious exception to all this ... so-called freedom. What about corruption? He [a journalist] might be killed. The media is afraid of officials so there's often no proper investigation. And there's even internet restrictions creeping in now, which are very worrying. The excuse is, they're saying they're protecting kids but that makes for any kind of excuse, we know that. It's easy to make a decision to block sites.
>
> [Asked to give an example, she points to the Fergana news agency website] This covered events in Osh, the violence and ... its origins, by providing a ... what you might call an ... alternative view and it got banned in Kyrgyzstan.

This was a fairly well-publicised example, however, of a Kyrgyz media clampdown, which received a degree of international attention and revolved around claims and counter-claims, which were inevitably controversial as, to an extent, interpretations depended on ethnicity (Fergananews.com, 2012). The Fergana website attempted an alternative analysis of events, which the participant claimed was more balanced, but given the difficulty of establishing verifiable facts in cases like these, the participant was asked to provide an alternative example which related to the general political situation in the country.

> Elena, Kyrgyzstan: The most important one I can think of is that in April 2010 the entire circulation of one particular newspaper was brought out by one person. That newspaper was about to cover, er, conversations between Kazak and Kyrgyz officials. Our PM has, let's say, too much business with the Kazaks. This stuff, these details, were about to be published. Everyone understands who it was, why it happened, but no one can say.

The interviewee was not prepared to give further details, beyond the implication that a member of the governing party, or one of its supporters, "brought out" the edition in question to prevent the revelations about his financial dealings going public, and the author was unable to verify this claim. However, this participant went on to outline more general structural problems in Kyrgyz journalism which again echoed the comments of many journalists in the other three countries but contrasted quite sharply with the views of the other Kyrgyz participants. The strong implication was that of journalistic self-censorship: particularly with regard to the reporting and exposure of corruption, a long-running issue in Kyrgyz public life and institutions which has been worsened by the unstable political climate. There is a notable contrast here with Georgia, for example, which was once notorious for corruption. Georgian leader Saakashvili famously replaced the entire Georgian police force shortly after assuming power following the Rose Revolution in an effort to stamp out endemic corruption (Caryl, 2012).

> Elena, Kyrgyzstan: It's not just the newspapers that do this. Look at our national TV channels. There's very little on corruption, virtually no mention of it. Yet, it's here, of course it's here … it's a major problem and it's widely discussed on social networks. And, you know what, they are trying to check online forums. Just as serious is the ownership issue. Owners of newspapers are … political. We can't cover events like journalists do in the UK and US. Papers are too expensive for people too, and sales have dropped because of websites. So some papers have started putting material online just on Friday.

Again, these responses contrast sharply with that of the other Kyrgyz participants, although all interviewees highlighted the problems of declining circulations but chose to place a different emphasis on them, as well as what they saw as the reasons for a lack of investigative journalism in the country.

> Begaim, Kyrgyzstan: The main problem is, er … lack of conditions in editorial offices. You know, finance, bad safety and so on [referring to poor standards of building and accommodation for journalists in Kyrgyzstan]. So it's often a resource issue when it comes to, say, the investigation of corruption. It's not a taboo – it's just that there aren't enough … investigators, resources.

A significant contextual difference between Kyrgyzstan and the other countries surveyed is that of geography and infrastructure. Kyrgyzstan is a mountainous country with an undeveloped infrastructure. Although not large in area, much of the country lies above 4,000 m: rising to over 7,000 m in the Tien Shan mountains on the border with China. This means that political life is overly centralised in Bishkek, despite significant regional centres like Osh, partly because those centres have a highly distinctive regional culture, with Osh characterised by its ethnic mix, a factor that has frequently resulted in violent inter-ethnic clashes during the post-Soviet era. Whilst this is not unusual, indeed Georgia and Armenia are also characterised by mountainous landscapes, difficult terrain and a political culture that is overly centralised in the capital city, Kyrgyzstan's serious economic problems and unusually awkward topography render communication outside the capital particularly difficult.

> Elena, Kyrgyzstan: There's a huge knowledge gap between Bishkek and rural areas. How are they supposed to keep in touch in the country ... outside the city? Maybe electricity is shut down ... that happens often. I think they strongly depend on the print press outside Bishkek, and of course not all Bishkek papers are distributed outside the city.

A more nuanced view was provided by another Kyrgyz participant, who requested full anonymity and had a tendency to occupy the "middle ground" between the buoyant optimists and the accusations of self-censorship and journalistic taboos characteristic of "Elena" when answering the first question about the barriers to the mainstream press.

> C, Kyrgyzstan: Well certainly I think that the press in Kyrgyzstan is relatively free, when compared to Russia or its Central Asian neighbours. Whether that has produced a

qualitative change in journalism over the years is another issue, however. Salaries at domestic papers and online resources are low – nearly always less than $500 per month, and that brings to bear on quality. Also, degrees of control exist at most outlets, as ... despite the fact that Kyrgyzstan's political society is more ... pluralistic, major political figures are behind nearly every media resource. The Kyrgyz-language newspaper *Sayasat*, for instance, is thought to be sponsored by Kamchibek Tashiyev, a nationalist opposition leader. The website 24.kg was rumoured to be controlled by Feliks Kulov [a former Prime Minister], and K-News [another website] is thought to be influenced to a degree by Omurbek Babanov. This results in those outlets offering their political patrons an ... umbrella during a storm, although this is not necessarily a criticism ... and, er, free interview opportunities and op-eds [opinion pieces] directed at their opponents.

This participant said that he had been carefully watching the results of the end of the libel laws, and their implications for journalism and politics in Kyrgyzstan.

C, Kyrgyzstan: As far as I have seen the end of the libel laws has not stopped politicians trying to sue newspapers that print what they consider to be misinformation about them. Whether it has resulted in fewer successful court verdicts I don't know. Just from Twitter I gleaned recently that Shirin Aitmatova (MP) had threatened to sue *Vecherni Bishkek* [an online newspaper]. Ismail Isakov [former defence minister] had promised to do the same and the Police Academy had threatened to sue *Delo Nomer* [another online newspaper – both Russian language – both based in Bishkek] for an article written about a drunken brawl at its graduation ceremony.

This journalist was asked about the coverage of corruption: specifically, whether there was a taboo surrounding its journalistic coverage and investigative journalism in particular.

C, Kyrgyzstan: Regarding corruption as a taboo, I would say that there is a little in the way of investigative journalism per se. Part of that is financial. If I am going to spend a few months following the cash trail of a highly-placed official, possibly one with connections to violent circles, I am going to want a decent salary to do so as compensation for the risks I am taking. In cases where this does happen, often an important opposition figure is picking up the tab for the journalist. An example of this was Omurbek Tekebayev paying Gennady Pavluk to investigate [former President] Kurmanbek Bakiyev and his family's corruption. In the end Pavluk was thrown out of a window in Kazakhstan, but I imagine his salary up until that point was many times bigger than the average newspaper journalist. Pavluk's material ended up on .ru [Russian] websites so I wouldn't discount the fact that he was being paid by the Kremlin, too, and rumours of ethnic Russian journalists being paid by Moscow abound here.

Finally, this journalist raised a point about the relationship between journalism and public relations in Kyrgyzstan. Whilst journalists in the other three countries mentioned "advertorials" as increasingly characterising contemporary print journalism, particularly in Ukraine, few highlighted it as an overarching barrier to conventional journalism in their countries. "C" claimed its effects were deeper and more significant in their political implications than many observers realised, although he ended on an optimistic note about the new generation of journalists in Kyrgyzstan.

C, Kyrgyzstan: Something which I think is particularly important here is the thin line between journalism and PR.

Shades of Expression

Again this comes down to cash and affects online resources less than newspapers – but it skews objectivity and represents a deep malaise in Kyrgyzstani journalism. I know one journalist, whose name I won't mention, who was quite open about having received money from a former Bakiyev business associate to write articles in a major national newspaper that would swing public opinion against the government's decision to take him to court in an international arbitration trial. To that particular business associate, a few thousand dollars would not be much to effectively control the tone of articles written about his business ventures in Kyrgyzstan. To the journalist it means having an iPad, an iPhone and being well-dressed. The young online journalists I know have an almost ideological stance against this sort of thing, and hopefully that isn't just connected to their youth.

CHAPTER 7

EVIDENTIAL: WHAT IS THE RELATIONSHIP BETWEEN ONLINE NEWS MEDIA, THE MAINSTREAM PRESS AND POLITICS?

A follow-up question, which asked interviewees to name particularly influential websites, was also posed where relevant, and absorbed in the results and analysis below: Are there any genuinely influential online political websites in your country?

The follow-up question was intended to draw out participants' views on what they saw as particularly influential political websites, although in all four countries several participants had already raised the issue by referring to particular independent news websites *before* this follow-up question was posed. Clearly, the subtext – not directly articulated by the interviewer – was linked to the first question about barriers to conventional journalism in Georgia, Armenia, Ukraine and Kyrgyzstan. Could any of these websites offer a "solution" to the mainstream deficiencies outlined previously? So, whereas Ukraine has obvious similarities with Russia and Belarus in terms of its internal cultural identity and historical development, its recent political trajectory and in particular the role of the media and civil society in the run-up to the Colour Revolutions has clear parallels with Georgia. Indeed, the Orange Revolution was even more closely associated with issues of media freedom, as the murder of prominent journalist Georgiy Gongadze (who was of Georgian origin) in 2000 remained a key focal point for the protests against the then President Leonid Kuchma. Gongadze had founded the *Ukrainska Pravda* website, discussed at length in the evidential chapters of this book, a few months before his death in an explicit attempt to circumvent government control over the media.

The millions of protestors involved in the Orange Revolution were also seeking a more general improvement in transparency and living standards. The responses to this question were perhaps the most notable, in the sense that almost every participant highlighted the existence of an independent "hub" news website seen as most influential. Every Ukrainian journalist, without exception, mentioned *Ukrainska Pravda* as the most notable online journal and several participants cited the website as the *only* exception to the rather dismal picture of Ukrainian journalism outlined in the first section above. Similarly, every Georgian journalist independently mentioned the *Netgazeti* website, again highlighting its independent, trusted status (*Liberali*, a similar Georgian site, was also frequently cited: it is also published as a conventional magazine). This response related to the overarching second question about the relationship between online journalism and the mainstream press (although most participants began by outlining access issues in the context of online journalism), with "hub" websites in all four countries not merely setting the mainstream agenda, or forming part of a wider news "source cycle" (cf. Messner and DiStasto, 2008), but often transcending mainstream journalism entirely.

The Georgians were slightly more likely to stress future potential rather than current activity, while the Ukrainians focused on a series of very recent developments which illustrated a wider truth about the political power of online journalism in that country. The Armenian participants highlighted two, sometimes three, key independent websites that they felt to be increasingly politically influential: again, however, there were signs that one of these was beginning to dominate in terms of audience and influence. In Kyrgyzstan, the evolution of online journalism is at a slightly earlier stage, and remains characterised by numerous sites competing for influence. However, because the independent print press in Kyrgyzstan is arguably even more fragmented than in the other three countries, and failed to evolve, in terms of influence, to the same extent in the post-Soviet era, there remain several equally influential news websites which have simply supplanted the print press in that country. In that sense, the role of online journalism in a rapidly evolving journalistic environment like Kyrgyzstan, where political reform and legislative change characterises a more general context of rapid democratisation, has obvious relevance as a means of engaging the public with these processes.

> Aslan, Kyrgyzstan: I work for an online news agency, but we sell, er, access to information, and we have ... agreements with print media to supply them with stories. The stories come from us, online, then they go to the print press. We used to have a printed newspaper, called [in English] "lemon", but we withdrew from that and went online ... because of the cost. It's all much, much cheaper online and, in Kyrgyzstan at least, it hasn't lost us any readers. Last month we recorded 450,000 unique visitors to the site, which gives you some idea of our potential influence. Around 70% of these were Kyrgyz. We have sites in three languages – Russian, Kyrgyz, English – but our Kyrgyz–language site is one of the most popular in Kyrgyzstan.

In a rapidly changing media environment, in a country like Kyrgyzstan in which democratic processes are evolving equally rapidly, online newspapers have clear influence. This was not always seen as a positive. Three Kyrgyz participants argued that the online press, in particular, had a tendency to *actively contribute* to political instability, and that the recent decision to dispense with libel laws had given all journalists – but those seeking a share of the fragmented online audience in particular – carte blanche to attempt to shape the political direction in which the country is heading. There was a suggestion from both these participants that online journalists resorted to rumour, often scurrilous, for political ends, and that news websites set the overall agenda by reporting the news well before the mainstream press in Kyrgyzstan.

> Kuban, Kyrgyzstan: Online is ... er ... out of control. You can write anything. It's becoming quite active ... very active in fact. Most information at the moment, about politics I mean, is online, certainly it's online first. Even the Russian-language news is the same. There are some news agencies that are the most trusted. When they publish something it attracts great attention. Readership of newspapers was reasonably high, I'd say, before the internet. But the web here has become very active in the past five years – you can find anything on the websites here.

The recent and continuing instability of Kyrgyzstan was cited by all participants in relation to the development of online journalism. Most felt that the media in Kyrgyzstan did a reasonable job of informing people, but opinion was split about the quality of the websites: some argued they were more measured and objective than newspapers, others felt that the Kyrgyz-language sites, in particular, were often overly partisan, which inevitably heightens tension among a politically aware and ethnically diverse population, given the country's recent history.

Aslan, Kyrgyzstan: Our society is ... very much politicised. When we sit round the table we talk ... too much politics. It's because of all the turbulence over the past five, ten, twenty years. People know, ah ... almost too much about politics. I certainly don't think that a big proportion of our population is excluded from that information, from political information, deliberately or not. TV news, state TV, now public TV and the internet in particular – they [the authorities] don't care so much about security any more, it's not like Soviet times. The opposition can speak openly on state TV and online. In fact maybe it's better to have security, er ... some security. With unrest, regime changes ... it's not good. You know, the recent regime change in 2010 ... then, the state disappears. You know, we hate the road police ... The ... traffic police, but when the regime changes we are suddenly happy to see them!

In other words, some evidence of functioning state institutions, even if they are corrupt and disliked, is a welcome sight at times of political instability. A chaotic and rapidly evolving online media sector finds itself in a position to thrive in such an environment, but also finds itself in a potentially highly influential position in terms of agenda setting and opinion forming. Indeed, web-based news media was banned from covering the October 2011 Kyrgyz Presidential elections: a clear governmental acknowledgement of its influence, with eleven news sites denied accreditation. Views on the validity of the ban were surprisingly mixed. Most of the participants tended to agree with the NGO "Progress in Kyrgyzstan", which argued that the decision "restricts the voters' rights to receive information about elections and constrains Presidential candidates" campaigning opportunities. Daniyar Karimov from the influential 24.kg website went further, suggesting that the decision could mark the beginning of "total censorship and an attempt to control [the] activities of information agencies" (Ismailov, 2011).

However, several of the participants took a different view, arguing that news websites cannot be absolved from the responsibilities that come with official accreditation as mass media organisations whilst continuing to produce (in some cases] inflammatory material.

> Joldosh, Kyrgyzstan: The state fails to calm people … but then they give the stage, er, I mean the media stage, to the opposition – who destabilise, they say, er … bad things. Then the state disappears, maybe because there's too much media freedom.

However, although some Kyrgyz interviewees were uncomfortable about the evolving role of online journalism in their country, their views were balanced: all pointed out that many sites, particularly what one journalist referred to as "portal" sites [what this book refers to as "hub" websites], were the most objective sources of Kyrgyz political news currently available. Indeed, the Kyrgyz authorities acknowledged this distinction when the Presidential elections took place in October 2011 by scaling back the initial blanket ban on web-based news agencies.

> C, Kyrgyzstan: The online portals are no more investigative than the newspapers, but tend to be more objective in reporting news. For "just the facts, ma'am", Kloop is an excellent organization, and their .kg office is relatively stronger than their .kz (Kazak) and .tj (Tajik) offices, partly because the media environment here is more favourable, but mostly because they run an excellent school here and the Kyrgyz graduates from the school are more in touch with it in terms of resources, follow-up training and so on.

Kloop is a Kyrgyz-centred news website, part funded by the Dutch Hivos organisation, that attracted a degree of global attention for its reportage of the 2010 unrest in Kyrgyzstan because the news is gathered and written by young journalists, many of whom are high school pupils. It has used crowdsourcing techniques, and also hosts hundreds of independent blogs.

In Georgia and Ukraine, responses to this question reflected the more mature media environment, in relative terms, compared to the fluidity of Kyrgyzstan. As such, responses revolved around structural barriers to the growth and spread of online journalism in environments where a once vibrant print press is declining to the point of insignificance, although political stability, or lack of it, remained an underpinning context, if not to the same extent.

> Nino R, Georgia: This coming year will be very important, I think, in terms of increasing online readership. Until last year there was a big war between rival internet providers [in Georgia] and now that war has been, ah ... handled by the government and now all are aiming at the regions and spreading out from just covering Tbilisi. We were working on a story about this recently, and we found out that all the regions will be covered by the end of this year and it, it ... won't be as expensive as it was a year or two ago so it will, you know, probably very soon become a serious alternative to many other kinds of news.

Using new media technologies as a "solution" to the problems inherent in existing mainstream news media environments is common in "West-facing" post-Soviet environments, but Hanitzsch et al. (2011) argue that the values of objectivity and impartiality have spread away from the "global North" in more general terms, and that

109

there are now often great similarities in role conceptions among journalists globally, although considerable differences in journalistic practices remain. This, they say, is especially true for the perceived importance of analysis, partisanship, entertainment and critical attitude towards the powerful. In all four countries, responses suggested that this change in "role conception" was expressing itself most clearly online. In other words conventional media, and newspapers in particular, were regarded by the participants as irrelevant and hopelessly dated, with a dwindling readership. In many cases, the participants argued that the mainstream press remained compromised by a still extant "Soviet mentality", and that Hanitzsch's point about changing values is most apparent online in the post-Soviet environment.

> Nana, Georgia: It's true that there's quite a bit of optimism around about the potential of web journalism in Georgia – there's a high standard of journalism, and it's often investigative and analytical in its, er ... tone. But I should also add that one of the big problems is low levels of access in the "regions" [areas outside Tbilisi]. At the moment it is only around 13–14%. This will go up this year, for sure.

This issue also characterises the situation in Armenia and Kyrgyzstan, where political power and economic development is also located overwhelmingly in the capital cities. There is, as a result, a form of democratic or communicative deficit whereby those in the capital city are far more likely to have web access than those in the "regions". In Ukraine, there is also a significant rural/urban split, with often very high levels of web access in Kiev. However, Ukraine's geography, and its large population, means that it has highly significant provincial cities like Donetsk,

110

Kharkov and Lviv, which all enjoy similarly high levels of web access. There is no equivalent to this in Georgia, Armenia or Kyrgyzstan, which are dominated culturally and politically by their capital cities, with few large provincial cities. And, as several participants pointed out, high levels of access do not necessarily mean that those who are active online are searching out political or even journalistic content.

> Maksym, Ukraine: There's no doubt that we have high levels of web access in Ukraine, around 50% in cities, maybe up to 60% in Kiev. A site like *Ukrainska Pravda* gets 200,000 daily visitors, which sounds impressive until you realise it's maybe 1.5% of the entire Ukrainian web audience, so it's not popular to use the web as a source of news.

> Nino, Georgia: Websites like *Liberali* and *Netgazeti* make a real attempt to provide balanced news. They're not popular with advertisers, and that's a real problem because they have to rely on meagre grants from NGOs. It's only a small number of Georgians who are using the internet to view political information so this is not going to be big business.

However, limited access is only a partial indicator of political influence. Indeed, the work of Megenta (2011) and Geniets (2011) suggests that the impact of the web should not be predicted by the number of people who use it. In contexts where online media remains the preserve of the educated middle class this can allow for the development of democratic social practices and information discourse online by reducing government control of information and enhancing political participation. Megenta (2011) explores the ways that online participatory media is chipping away at the power of overtly authoritarian regimes in sub-Saharan Africa, for example, arguing that the democratisation of elite groups in authoritarian contexts can trigger wider social and political changes. Equally significantly, early adopters of the technology often set its future direction: for Megenta, they have an interpretative role in the evolution of that media technology. In Tunisia, for example, well before the events of the Arab Spring the earliest users of web-based media were often liberals with anti-authoritarian views (Abrougui, personal correspondence, 2012). It becomes, therefore, a subversive medium.

In Ukraine and Georgia, despite very different economic and cultural contexts, a similar pattern emerges. Anti-government protests in Georgia during 2011 were covered at length on the *Netgazeti* site, and *Ukrainska Pravda* is well-known for its independent stance and scepticism towards political elites. Coverage on both sites often contrasts with the silence of the mainstream press: there is, in other words, an increasing tendency for these online hub websites to simply sidestep the mainstream press. The "source cycle" is less noticeable: instead there is a coalscing of interested and engaged readers around trusted online sources. Although these readers may be small in number, they are influential, and there is also the potential for those numbers to increase dramatically when the political situation dictates a wider interest.

> Vitaly, Ukraine: There's definitely a correlation between the overall political situation in Ukraine and the audience's interest in web-based news. There is a zeitgeist. Google summaries prove this. Most users are just interested in, er, you know … celebrity news and gossip but at number 10 in the list of search terms in Ukraine is still Tymoshenko

[jailed former Prime Minister], even though the issue has gone away from the mainstream. Maybe 10% of Ukrainian web users are engaged in political issues most of the time.

Geniets (2011) considers further the specifics of this access argument, which is frequently cited by those cynical about the democratising potential of new media. She argues we are witnessing the rise of a global elite and in many countries "cosmopolitans do not consume the same information about the world as their fellow citizens" (Geniets, 2011, p. 74). Similarly, Megenta (2011) argues that although overtly authoritarian regimes like that of Ethiopia censor the web, its cyberspace is highly subversive because those who have access are generally anti-government. In the context of Ukraine and Georgia a small number of influential blogs have the majority of inward links, giving early adopters enormous power to further interpret and reinterpret journalistic use of the web. One Ukrainian participant felt this would lead to more influential local content in conjunction with the development of a national independent "hub" site.

> Maksym, Ukraine: Online websites are in a very interesting position. Any bad news about the Ukrainian authorities is very popular, er, news spreads fast. And it is going local, or maybe even hyperlocal. There are two or three big local news sites at present but I think the future will be local. Ukrainian online journalism is mainly copycat journalism apart from *Ukrainska Pravda*, whereas local news can generate real news and interest.

Megenta (2011) notes that the relationship between bloggers and the mainstream media in African authoritarian countries is much less fractious, both rhetorically and in practice, than in the West. Bloggers both directly and indirectly influence the agenda of mainstream media outlets and they also function as agenda-testing grounds for journalists. Roberts (2011) argues that, in some deficient media contexts, distinctive small-scale "source cycles" are emerging, which implicitly (often explicitly) recognise the failure of the traditional mainstream press and set about developing an alternative. This recognition of deficiency, and the deliberate attempt to address it, is crucial. Indeed, Atton and Hamilton (2011) define the concept of "alternative journalism" as being informed by a critique of existing ways of doing journalism. It proceeds both from dissatisfaction with the mainstream coverage of topics but also with the epistemology of news, emphasising, for instance, alternative sourcing routines and the subordinate role of audience as receiver.

Such an approach means that online journalism finds itself able to set a wider media agenda, with far-reaching implications. Messner and DiStasto (2008) argue that newspapers are increasingly legitimising blogs as credible sources, identifying a mutually beneficial "source cycle" between the two in their US-based research. In this model, blogs rely heavily on traditional media as sources, while the mainstream press is increasingly inclined to legitimise blogs as credible sources of information, particularly in the political realm. As it applies to US journalism, it is perhaps inevitable that this model suggests that, although blogs can "create a buzz" around issues, this only reaches a limited public until it is then re-sourced by the traditional media.

In smaller-scale and/or structurally deficient media environments, like Ukraine and Georgia, but even more notably in Armenia and Kyrgyzstan, these relationships are less skewed in favour of the mainstream press. Indeed, until the Arab Spring, the Anglocentrism which characterised debate about the democratising potential of new media had the inevitable effect of underestimating or misconstruing that potential. Even in the post-Arab Spring context, this parochialism means that interpretations of the role of new media tend to be unhelpfully narrow in scope. Comparative approaches argue, in contrast, that the most valid and substantive way to assess the impact and reach of political blogs is to consider their relationship with the mainstream news agenda. This approach contends that smaller-scale media contexts offer some unique opportunities for online journalism to gain traction by impacting on, and enriching, the wider public sphere. Reese, Rutigliano, Hyun and Jeong (2009) argue that the impact of blogs is enhanced by anchoring their discussions to the stream of information, opinion and analysis produced by traditional media. Similarly, Drezner and Farrell (2004) argue that if a critical number of high-profile blogs raise a particular story, it can attract the interest of mainstream media outlets. If the mainstream media therefore address and frame critical issues, which political actors feel obliged to address, independent online journalism can perhaps construct focal points through which the mainstream media choose to operate. A significant critical mass needs to develop around blogs of this kind if they are to succeed in attracting the attention of the mainstream media, however. The obvious corollary to this is: to what extent can participatory media drive civic engagement? The figures are not encouraging but, as Megenta (2011) argues, such active participants are always likely to be in the minority. What matters is for new and diverse voices to join the debate and help provide a catalyst for others.

Ruslan, Ukraine: When the Tymoshenko issue happened there was some discussion on TV but all that is censored so people double check information online. I think they ... more rely on the web. They trust it more because there's a variety of opinions, um ... there's always people for and against. People are a little bit tired of the way TV reports because often they show one-sided arguments. Even people who are not active, who say they're not interested, suddenly get interested in something like the Tymoshenko case. People get clips from the web, you know ... they, er, find things out. Web users ridiculed Yanukovych when a wreath blew into his face during a sombre ceremony. The creativity of users brings irony into political discussion and this, um, is an important ... a vital point. I believe that it's humour that makes the web powerful in Ukraine, because with TV and the press satire is just not a developed genre here. Satirical creativity ... that's what I mean and the, er, web lets people communicate with each other. They're not under time pressure in quite the same way ... they don't always have particular objectives.

The importance of political satire in the "new" context of online journalism, and its potential to engage the audience by simply sidestepping the more cautious mainstream media was further developed by another Ukrainian participant.

Yevhen, Ukraine: Satire has hugely contributed to the success of online in Ukraine. Social media is full of satirical treatments. It's just a pity that some people who don't use social media are cut out of the loop. You must have heard of the mobile phone footage of the Yanukovych "wreath incident" [the same incident referred to by Ruslan above, in which the wind blew a ceremonial wreath towards the Prime Minister's face at a commemorative service]. In half an hour it went viral despite his attempts to "manage the

crisis" by deleting footage. The PM is, I would say ...
dyslexic in terms of expressing his ideas and people have
fun exploiting that online. Journalists in traditional media
wouldn't be able to do this. Here the government is not
playing the same game as it is in Russia. Here they don't
understand how powerful the web is. Either you use it for
its own sake or you try to control it.

In journalistic terms, the immediacy of interactive debate,
the "cultural terrain of cyberspace", has several distinct
technology-derived advantages over the mainstream press.
Not least of these is the potential to capture the features of
dialogue more robustly than print and the potential to
collapse spatial boundaries, as well as engaging readers via
satire and other popular forms of journalism and reportage.
While this may be a less notable benefit in the Anglosphere,
in the post-Colour Revolution environments analysed here
web-based journalism allows for alternative perspectives to
make a considerable impact and gain a considerable audience. Further to this, Lasica (2003) highlights the dynamism
of web-based interactivity. When journalism becomes a
process, not a static product, audiences discard their traditional role as passive consumers of news and become
empowered partners with a shared stake in the end result.
Blogs are the most powerful and accessible current tool for
user-generated content, and illustrate most clearly the
changing nature of the relationship between producers and
consumers of news. As Sambrook (2006) and others argue,
the appeal of blogging as a counterpoint to mainstream
reporting is readily apparent, especially when set against
the current tendencies towards homogeneity and standardisation which increasingly characterise market-driven
journalism.

Vitaly, Ukraine: New media is becoming our key priority – we teach journalists how to use new media technologies. New voices are being raised in Ukraine, who also know that the web may bring profits. It's true that for many new media is just a hobby but they want to be professionals. I, er, think I'd go so far as to say we have a developing community of media innovators. Their motivation isn't primarily to report independently but rather, um, a chance to work as journalists. They may be critical and will share information that shows government weakness. Bear in mind too that web access here is a lot cheaper here than it is in the Baltic States, say. Access is easy to obtain. Critical mass has already been reached among the young but it's also high with the middle aged.

Yevhen, Ukraine: More and more people consider online news their main source of media, you know, we didn't have an enormous culture of print media, so a ... niche was open. In the vacuum of independent Ukraine no quality newspapers emerged. We only had local newspapers or tabloid style newspapers. Magazines are a huge market, yes, but it was, er, new media that really filled the gap.

Nino R, Georgia: I'd have to say that, already in certain communities online news is the only news they have. Someone already mentioned minorities, well that is a good example – although of course these people are often accessing websites from outside Georgia. I don't know the numbers but many people just don't watch TV, especially the news, and they don't read newspapers ... but they are very informed. Social networks like Facebook are definitely being used to, erm, counteract problems in mainstream press. And I think we are using these sites more and more for social reasons than private. People choose friends based on who has the most and best information, who are the news givers.

Nana, Georgia: I think in terms of online journalism this year is also important for a second reason, which is a big US aid grant to assist Georgian media. They have a huge emphasis, a huge aim, to assist online new media development so there will be some big-scale grants given to local and regional media outlets to develop online media channels. So I think this will change the media landscape here.

Begaim, Kyrgyzstan: All the information from online publications is used by all other journalists, whether it is newspaper, TV or radio. So we see the influence of internet news on public opinion in Kyrgyzstan, or Bishkek at least, growing every day. New media can ... replace, or ... make our public more aware. Whether this is good or bad I don't know.

The participants all had a tendency to swap terms when referring to the democratising potential of online journalism. This is significant as there is a considerable, and growing, issue regarding the definition of terms in the area of new media and online journalism. In particular, when attempting to make an assessment of the potential for online journalism to promote meaningful political change, precise definitions are of fundamental importance. Lievrouw (2011) argues that "new media" has become something of a cultural "place-holder". People often use it without having a clear idea of what it means, partly because the boundaries of new media are often uncertain. More recently, the use of social media and other online forms during the Arab Spring encapsulated the importance of the "network" as a means of countering the traditional dominance of political elites in environments where those elites see the media as something to be "controlled". As such, much of this sort of online journalism could be considered alternative or activist.

> David, Georgia: We all use Facebook to discuss issues and ideas. There are over 600,000 users in Georgia. Interestingly our neighbours Armenia tried to mirror the Arab Spring and organise some kind of Facebook Revolution. It didn't really work but it says something about the potential for online activism of this kind in the [Caucasus] region. Look, when the mainstream can't provide you with reliable or meaningful information you search for substitutions. There is a need for different perspectives.

Lievrouw (2011) attempts to define alternative and activist new media as employing or modifying the communication practices and social arrangements of new information technologies to challenge or alter dominant, accepted ways of reporting and engaging in society, culture and politics. The networked nature of new media allows creators, via the ubiquity and interactivity it offers users, to create projects in which people share information, extend networks and contacts, and critique or intervene in prevailing social, cultural, economic and political conditions. New media of this kind do not only reflect or critique mainstream media and culture, they constitute and intervene in them. Much of this echoes the more recent views of Mason who argues that the events of the Arab Spring demonstrate conclusively the power of the network and its ability to defeat or challenge political elites (Mason, 2012, Lievrouw, 2011). In the Ukrainian context, although participants argued that the authorities did not recognise the political power of the web to the extent of their Russian counterparts, they did suggest that increased efforts to control it might come in the near future. They also highlighted the critical trend for hub websites to mobilise social media: in effect, to play an editorial role and bring activist debate to a wider audience.

Yevhen, Ukraine: Last week a file service was closed down in Ukraine. Officially we were told this was because of piracy but next day 100,000 people organised to attack government websites and closed them down. This was all organised by social networks and publicised by *Ukrainska Pravda*. The government were paralysed in web terms but they were particularly upset because they couldn't control the situation … and they eventually reinstated the pirate service. But, you know what, it's a pyrrhic victory for us, because the government may try to devote more effort now to control the web, more like they do in Russia. This could be really dangerous at some point in the near future and could bring tighter controls over the web in general.

Ruslan, Ukraine: Now, for all public campaigns the best way is to use social networks. We realise that if we're united we can send a message to government. The Tymoshenko debate took place mostly online, and I'm not sure this was appreciated internationally. But Twitter is still a weak instrument here … Facebook is the number one place to consume news. And I should add that the Pravda news site helps coordinate it all, or at least publicises what's going on, makes it … central.

Participatory journalism such as that referenced by the interviewees seeks to critique and reform the press by involving "amateur" reporters in the practice of journalism. It becomes an interactive process, and adopts the forms of professional journalism but with the purpose of transforming the press as an institution. It provides new arenas for news opinion and analysis that is marginalised by the mainstream. Newman's (2009) study of how UK and US mainstream media is responding to the wave of participatory social media and the historic shift in control towards individual consumers, argues that social media, blogs and user-generated content are not replacing journalism, but are creating an important extra layer of information and diverse opinion. Most people are still happy to rely on mainstream news organisations to sort fact from fiction and serve up a filtered view, but they are increasingly engaged by this information, particularly when recommended by friends or another trusted source. He concludes that there is a new confidence in the underlying values of journalism and the role that social media might play in keeping those values relevant in the digital age: in this sense, "hub" websites like those cited by the participants offer the benefits of some form of editorial "filtering" whilst retaining the open and diverse qualities of web-based analysis.

As recently as 2008, however, Kung et al. felt able to claim that the internet has had "remarkably little impact" on the types and formats of content that is presented to audiences. Online newspapers, they argued, may provide individual articles rather than news pages, but these articles tend to be identical to the ones published in the print paper. Further, new content is scarce and new content formats even scarcer. Not only does this seem, again, to be a highly Anglocentric analysis, but even in that context it would seem an inaccurate generalisation. In the UK, for example, *The Guardian*'s website had been innovating in terms of content, format, and separation from the print newspaper for several years by 2008.

Other writers have focused on blogging for their criticisms of the effectiveness of new media forms, sometimes perpetuating the old polarity by arguing that blogging contains the power to become a valuable tool in online publishing and as a historical archive, but instead has created another avenue for media saturation of the self. Potentially it could become a worldwide forum for an e-democracy and dissent but, according to Smith (2008) it has "disappointed in this aspiration". Previous criticisms have centred on literary merit, she adds, while actually the greatest flaw of the blog discourse is the overinvestment in the self rather than an outward discussion of the world.

By contrast, Perlmutter (2008) adopts an evangelical approach that perhaps goes too far in the opposite direction, again highlighting the old polarity that has been comprehensively debunked in recent years, arguing that [blogging's] medium, venue and style heralded a wave of interactive technologies that continues to change our society, culture and politics: "It's the province of people who are passionate about politics, policies and public affairs and will work to change the world" (p. 205). Perlmutter concedes that blogs tend to be partisan, but argues that this is largely because those involved want to provide alternative perspectives: "Unless you buy them off they cannot be controlled from above ... The essence of understanding blog interactivity is its personal relationship building. Blogs have achieved greatness, they are not a fad, and will become part of almost every political campaign."

Writing in the context of the US, Perlmutter's views chime with several of the Ukrainian participants, in particular, by suggesting that although blogging "fame" is often related to high-profile, national stories, there are many smaller bloggers who are specialise in focusing on issues on the local level. Bloggers, he argues, are performing many political education functions by creating dialogues where previously there were only top-down monologues and infusing new energy into the analysis of both local and national government. The Ukrainian participants echoed much of Perlmutter's evangelical analysis, suggesting that local blogs have a real political and educative function in provincial Ukrainian cities: but the wider truth of such analysis is revealed by the dominance of national hub websites, where local blogs often form part of the collation process, in which myriad sources, often collated by amateurs, are marshalled into something with real influence by the professional journalists behind blogs like *Ukraianska Pravda* and Georgia's *Netgazeti*.

In dysfunctional media environments, where the mainstream media cannot or will not "serve up a filtered view" of this interactivity and participation, this coalescing around hub websites, those which deliberately position themselves as an alternative to mainstream journalism but do this via a rather traditional, objective approach, the kind of journalism fetishised as the Western ideal, seems more significant and is illustrated by some of the examples from participants outlined below. We know that the net allows diverse groups to coordinate and organise protests in a very short time. But there are more significant political developments in Ukraine and Georgia, and to a lesser extent Armenia and Kyrgyzstan, whereby a particular, professionally produced but independent site deliberately addresses mainstream deficiencies by providing a focal point for the discontented and a "filtered", often edited, source of social media. This is a crucial distinction, and one that is frequently overlooked in Anglocentric interpretations of new media's potential – both by those on the evangelical side of the argument, like Perlmutter, and the more cynical perspectives of Smith and Kung et al.

> Tetyana, Ukraine: The recent tax protests in Kiev were interesting. It was the first genuine protest since the Orange Revolution in my view. Basically, small businesses were protesting over tax, just ordinary people. They, erm, debated the issues online then gathered in Maidan [Kiev's main square]. In fact it spilled over from online to offline. Mainstream media was so reluctant to cover it that people had to go online to cover it ... to read about it even. These aren't people who know how to use Facebook and Twitter, they're market traders. Instead they used simple online forums. The protests went on for a whole day before TV channels mentioned it. New media pushed the mainstream media to cover it. Someone took webcam footage and published it online. It was almost as if we all participated. Then even the international media covered it before the Ukrainian media. Our media was waiting, waiting to cover it. Suddenly you see a live community gathering online and, bang, we all know about it. No one trusts the [mainstream] media so we look for comments from the, er ... guy next door. There's always the question whether these professional journalists have some kind of agenda. This is why *Ukrainska Pravda* is a key source of news and information. It collates this stuff, it's reliable and it puts it all into some kind of journalistic focus ... I follow bloggers who are not journalists. The big difference between Ukraine and Russia is that we don't have blogging "faces". There are so many bloggers, loads of bloggers, but no "faces". I always come across new bloggers – they don't have ties between them, no aggregation. It's almost like we're walking round in the dark and then you suddenly stumble across something. I think that's a big reason for the success ... the ... value, of a more professional site like *Ukrainska Pravda*.

This participant highlighted differences between Ukraine and Russia. The contextual presence of Russia is obviously critical when discussing Ukrainian, Armenian, Kyrgyz and Georgian politics. Vladimir Putin has spent much time and energy attempting to recreate a sphere of influence in the Caucasus, Central Asia and parts of Eastern Europe. Although formally a democracy, Russia has well-documented strong authoritarian tendencies under his leadership (Garton Ash, 2004). However, Russia's internet space, Runet is virtually free of censorship or government control and, unlike China, Russia has not created an internet framework it can easily control. Indeed, the BBC covered Russian opposition use of the *LiveJournal* blogging platform in March 2012 (Greenall, 2012). The changing media landscape in Russia is crucial in explaining the growth of opposition sentiment in the country. Since 2007 the number of Russian internet users has jumped from 23 to 53 million; more than 13 million use Facebook and the old media are now easily bypassed (*The Week*, 2012). Fossato and Lloyd (2008), however, argue that Russian online networks are often "closed and intolerant" with web users unresponsive to political campaigning online. The context of Russia is crucial for the four countries studied here, as elements in all four countries frequently define themselves in opposition to it. The size of the Russian media sector, however, renders comparisons unhelpful and it inevitably results in a more fragmented online news environment, a chaotic pluralism: indeed, this study as a whole argues that "large-scale" media environments like that of Russia limits the impact of online political journalism, but that in other contexts and cultures, with smaller-scale media environments, web-based journalism remains a serious, and sometimes lone, challenge to the failings of the mainstream press. And, further, that "hub" websites provide a focus for interested parties. That said, financing online political journalism of this nature is likely to remain a challenge, another major thrust of the interviewees' responses.

> Katarina, Georgia: The journal *Liberali*, especially the web version, and the purely online *Netgazeti*, are good examples of the kind of publication that advertisers stay away from in Georgia. They do this because of the content ... it's truthful, real journalism. But they struggle, you know, financially. The main source of income for both are grants provided by international NGOs for the development of independent media. Income from this is tiny though.

This is a critical issue. The journal *Liberali*, a serious publication in both online and print forms, is committed to independent political journalism but is effectively forced to depend on small grants from international donors to stay afloat. Advertising revenue is essentially non-existent, with all Georgian participants and *Liberali* journalists claiming that the reason is political. In short, advertisers do not want to be associated with *Liberali* or *Netgazeti* because of the political content. Similarly, in Ukraine, *Ukrainska Pravda* has frequently been a focus of government attention. Indeed, it was refused press accreditation in 2002. It, too, struggles for advertising revenue and is partially dependent on small grants from international donors, although not to the extent of the Georgian titles.

In Armenia, a somewhat different situation prevails, with some online websites accused of a form of benevolent plagiarism: essentially copying stories from mainstream newspapers. As mentioned in section one, newspapers in Armenia are largely subsidised by political parties and, according to the interviewees, have little motivation or interest in attracting readers. As a result, this form of plagiarism is allowed to continue, with many of those websites then revamping those stories to attract more readers.

B, Armenia: Online websites are killing papers too. They pick the best stories and cover them themselves. They sometimes run them uncut but ... more often they'll pick up the stories and put their own spin on them. The papers don't care. This proves, better than anything else I think, that they're not ... we're not ... in a "market situation".

One of the Armenian participants worked as a journalist on the US-funded Radio Liberty, a combined web/radio operation. Again, there are obvious similarities with Ukraine and Georgia in the sense that some of the most influential websites are essentially subsidised by foreign donors. All of them stress their neutrality and independence from government, but that neutrality is inevitably somewhat compromised by the source of funding.

Artur, Armenia: Our journalists prepare their work for radio then reorganise for the online version ... our website. The web editor then disseminates the stories to Twitter, Facebook and so on. Our audience is biggish but not huge ... I think it's just in the top 10 of news websites, but that's not the main thing. The main thing is that we are really influential. Our site is taken as God's truth. The Armenian government has no influence on us, our funding comes from elsewhere.

My private observations are that people say to me: "you guys tell the truth". Our radio audience has 10% of Armenian news coverage. People listen to the radio then check it out with the website, and it's a highly political website. We have this mission to fill the gap. We focus on the stuff where people would otherwise be denied objective information, so we avoid sports, celebrities ... all that stuff, all that "yellow journalism". We don't go public with our statistics so we don't damage the market – we don't do advertising so we don't need to worry.

Omnik, Armenia: Whatever the online media outlets might claim, the statistics show us that the number of readers remains low. The number of online users has increased significantly, yes that's true. But this has not manifested itself in a huge surge in readers. That said, it is still much higher than the number of people that read newspapers.

This last point illustrates the importance of ensuring that these issues are not interpreted from an Anglocentric perspective: numbers of online news readers may be low, but it remains "much higher" than those reading news-papers. Several of the Armenian participants anticipated that this would lead to political problems, and highlighted what they saw as potential future interference with the most influential websites, claiming they had already detected some evidence of this.

Artur, Armenia: One issue in future that we have to be very careful about is that there might be closer monitoring of news websites as they become more influential. It's true ... I think, to say that online is coming under more scrutiny already. One high-profile website packed in because they were under too much pressure when they became in-fluential. Self-censorship is creeping in too, creeping into online journalism I mean. Radio Liberty is one of the few objective websites. One website was taken to court recently – Hraparak.com – for online comments. They did a story about a lawyer and readers' comments got them into trouble. For quite a while people were nervous. We just don't have legislation yet to cover this kind of thing.

The threat is still there. I am a prolific blogger, for instance. I have thousands of comments and some of these are potentially offensive – how could I possibly moderate all the comments? I'd have to quit my job. The sphere is not regulated properly.

An obvious example of this lack of regulation is the habit of some of Armenia's most popular news websites to simply lift stories from the small circulation newspapers. This is the flipside of an unfettered, unregulated web policy, although all participants felt this illustrated a wider problem with the Armenian media: subsidised newspapers were not concerned about the plagiarism, as their circulation figures are low and they are funded by their political masters. Rather, the interviewees felt that the tendency of these sites to pursue quantity rather than quality was the key issue.

Artur, Armenia: There are three main websites in Armenia: News.am, tert.am, 1in.am. These guys, like tert.am, came in with lots of money, they published like crazy … but it was yellow journalism, you know, 70–100 stories a day. By comparison we were doing 20 stories but it was all relevant stuff. These guys were, instead, doing it by quantity, volume. All three of these sites would copy our stuff, they take it from everywhere … they even launch different language versions. I think Russian, Turkish.

B, Armenia: Politicians only understand the figures so you have this strange situation where they publish like crazy. Radio Liberty, or any quality news website can't afford to do the same, nobody can humanly absorb all this information. These guys have little or no editorial policy – they don't prioritise much!

Artur, Armenia: Eventually we had a word with them and they do now start to prioritise important stories on their website and so increase their influence.

Some editorial control is now exerted. The Armenian participants were then asked the follow-up question about whether that meant there had been a general increase in journalistic quality online, and specifically whether any equivalents of Ukraine's *Ukrainska Pravda* or Georgia's *Liberali* were emerging.

Gegham, Armenia: Yes, I think Aravot is one site that is becoming more genuine – they try to generate their own stories and tackle some big issues. Hrapak now produce a different print and online version, while A1+ is now completely web based. It was the leader till 2010, but it lost its position to news.am, tert.am and 1in.am. Look, though, this is mainly gossip, scandal ... yellow stuff.

There's huge competition in that field too. They really try to increase their readership, they have ads, they have grants from different sources. They cover everything: politics as well as gossip, yellow journalism. They have a huge output with hundreds of stories, they translate into other languages for the diaspora and to increase readership. They're politically neutral too – you can prove nothing. There's rumours that news.am, the biggest website, is connected with ... let's say the authorities, but you can prove nothing. Self-censorship is still an issue though, even online.

Sonya, Armenia: The May [2012] elections will be an ... examination, let's say, for online journalism in Armenia. There's still a lack of web penetration here. Yes, we have sites like A1+ with 10–20,000 readers a day, and you have sites like Aravot which are beginning to have a real influence, a ... political influence, especially in Yerevan. Now there's maybe 40% web penetration in Yerevan, so they have to pass this "exam" when the election comes, to let the public see that online is a way of, er ... getting informed.

I'm not a huge fan of online media here – it's not always accurate, not always diverse. It can be "yellow" ... it lacks analysis. They're not ideal and they have some way to go. Aravot is probably the most analytical and the most influential. The main problem, I think, is that our media is acting apart, aside from, the economy, almost as if it is ... not connected. We are not in a healthy economic environment. We have to change the whole country to have independent and fair media but for now online is more independent and more uncensored. But they do have to be more professional, I have to say that.

The May 2012 elections in Armenia, which took place two months after the interviews, were indeed characterised by the use of new media, but this was most effective when it took the form of "monitorial" forms of citizen engagement. In April 2012, for example, a project called iDitord (Observer) was launched to monitor pre-electoral and election day processes by gathering information from civic activists from all over the country about electoral violations (Internews, 2012). The election also marked an upsurge in the political use of social media and visits to the hub websites cited by the participants, but this was not on the scale that some of the interviewees had hoped and anticipated: although it eclipsed the traditional print media (S. Petrosian, personal communication, 10 June 2012).

Another participant in Armenia continued the theme: as with the other Armenian participants, he was highly critical of the traditional print media in the country, but he also specifically linked its decline to the growth in online journalism, rather than more diffuse external economic or political factors.

> Davit, Armenia: Print media is ... regressing here, you could say. And this is *because* of online media, it's because of it. We have 100 news websites already and, do you know, only 10 national papers. Local websites are now generating their own news. Gyumri [the second largest city in Armenia] has one influential news website of its own, publishing its own news. This is a long way from the "cut and paste" model we used to see here. It's the first time here in Armenia that I can think of a local site doing this, but I know there's also news sites in Vanadzor and elsewhere. Other towns still mainly use Yerevan or Gyumri sites.

This participant identified the same websites – news.am, tert.am, 1in.am, Aravot – as the most influential. He also suggested that there was a developing tendency for web journalism to focus on analysis and news, whilst print concentrated on interviews.

> Davit, Armenia: As far as I'm concerned, these are all completely independent websites and Aravot [a leading newspaper] has also transferred to a website. I mean, it's still a paper but it now has an online edition. With Aravot, I'm seeing that the print version is focused on interviews with web focused on analysis and breaking news. The most interesting, er, significant ... thing is that people are using websites for news. Our papers are still linked to political parties, they always have been, but the web is more or less independent. The sites are mainly launched by people, ah, educated in the West. They fund themselves by grants, UNDP, major donors, plus gradually advertisers come,

133

then they gradually become sustainable. It's all self-regulating, self-sustaining let's say.

All the Armenian participants independently mentioned the political use of social media as growing in importance, suggesting that this was often collated and mobilised by influential websites, as with *Ukrainska Pravda* in Ukraine, as journalistic "source material". It is also, as in numerous other global contexts, increasingly used by politicians themselves as a means of circumventing, or attempting to circumvent, the independent media.

Omnik, Armenia: Social media, and especially Twitter has more power here than is perhaps usual in other countries. The PM has his Facebook page and the education minister does too – he uses Facebook to openly criticise, let's say. Politics is more and more open in Armenia – dialogues and discussion especially, and it's getting more open because of the web, because of social networks. Twitter is becoming more influential and the print media are all active on Facebook themselves.

Davit, Armenia: Overall, for me, it's definitely a positive picture. Online is becoming more … popular, even universities are starting special disciplines, like courses in web journalism. People starting websites are directed to what you might call civic journalism sites, people are willing to help, they see the value in this stuff. There's a site called pjc.am which helps them set things up.

Gagik, Armenia: Online has of course contributed to political openness and alternative forums, you know, and … frank discussion. The government cannot crack down, even if they wanted to they understand that if they tried to it wouldn't, er, bring them benefits. The government understands the … move towards the EU, towards their way of doing things. They can't control it, they know that if they tried they would get the attention of Europe. It knows it needs to do this, let it go free. This is very important for Armenia and Armenian society. Many initiatives are now organised through social media, like environment protests. The opposition want to use this as a propaganda tool but basically it's been used for environmental protests, single issue stuff, like elsewhere I think. It's political but it's not party political.

Davit, Armenia: I'd say we're getting more and more liberal in terms of media freedom, largely because of progress online and the difficulty of controlling the message online. Compared to Kocharyan [former President] times now it is ... heaven. Then it was hard work. Now, it may not be completely free but it's better than it was. They [authorities] understand that if they keep, er ... pressing on online media and political media they won't succeed internationally – look at Iran, one of our neighbours after all, look at Georgia even.

Sonia, Armenia: When business people control the media and are linked to the regime. Armenians know how all this looks internationally – maybe because of the diaspora.

As with the previous question, Kyrgyz journalists tended to have different perspectives on these issues. Again, the political instability that has characterised Kyrgyzstan over recent years is crucial context, offering opportunities as well as potential pitfalls for online journalism. Two of the Kyrgyz journalists chose to make a comparison with Georgia's post-Rose Revolution experience at the outset. One participant went on to independently outline a number of influential websites as the sector begins to consolidate.

Shades of Expression

C, Kyrgyzstan: There is definite evidence of a switch to online news in terms of popularity among the young, but this may take a decade or more to have political influence. Georgia feels like a younger society than Kyrgyzstan, partly because the Saakashvili administration that took power after the Rose Revolution was full of young people. In Kyrgyzstan now, there are definitely online operations doing some good things. AKIpress (online) and *Vecherni Bishkek* (paper) are thought relatively neutral, but this is a change that has occurred since Bakiyev's ousting. In fact, some have speculated that VB's editor is still doing Bakiyev's bidding as some of the criticism levelled at the current government is extremely harsh! K-news to my knowledge came after Bakiyev while Kloop suffered various threats during the Bakiyev period and saw its popularity spike during the revolution, as the government shut other resources down first. I would say that these four resources, and occasionally 24.kg are the most trustworthy in Kyrgyzstan.

Azmanbek, Kyrgyzstan: Kyrgyzstan is more free than Ukraine and Georgia. I can explain. After [former President] Bakiyev there was much freedom, then they suddenly all realise they're in power and soon start to control the flow of information. Bakiyev then tries to control everything and it suddenly becomes hard [for journalists] to work. A big propaganda team, including his son, get to work and for a while things are bad. Then the regime changed, they see the mistakes of Bakiyev – I think that they see that controlling the media would be harmful. Now it's big news if the authorities *ever* visit journalists, ever put pressure on. Even in Kazakhstan there's a very different atmosphere and especially in Uzbekistan – I had the opportunity to go there but didn't.

Another Kyrgyz participant continued the optimistic theme, also suggesting that online journalism within the country was responsible for a more general improvement in journalistic standards. This participant gave his perspective on quality, audience and influence as a journalist straddling the mainstream/online divide in Kyrgyzstan.

> Aslan, Kyrgyzstan: There is a clear tendency towards analytical, professional and detailed news – it's not just gossip, and that's very true online. I've followed the ... er, processes ... in Kyrgyz journalism, and it's developing very fast. Ten years ago nobody used the web for news. Now, its influence has become very important.
>
> I can give you plenty of examples of this. Look, some news in print media just gets, er, lost. But on our website it has a big impact. This could be ... is probably ... because of newspaper ownership – they're often not trusted, government newspapers are still, I would say, a Soviet legacy and they have a limited readership. People trust us. So if a story has a limited impact in newspapers it is much more serious if it's carried on our news site.

> Dina, Kyrgyzstan: Akipress is the most influential site in Kyrgyzstan. But it's like in business, I think. A small company starts to grow then begins to dominate ... but it can die one day. It's like ... the life cycle.

The Kyrgyz journalists acknowledged the fact that online journalism in the country was in a state of flux, yet in such a rapidly evolving journalistic environment there are still signs of a coalescing around one or two hub websites which begin to act as a form of public sphere for a small number of politically engaged readers. As in Armenia, Kyrgyz journalists all referenced what they saw as the ineptitude of the mainstream press, which allowed for online news agencies and the like to gain a foothold more easily than might be the case in more mature and evolved media environments.

Aslan, Kyrgyzstan: We [as web journalists] think we have to be flexible, mobile, open to new ideas. In the past our competitors were state news, state agencies. It was easy to be better than them ... it was easy to be more trusted than them in the early days after the end of the Soviet Union, and even more recently to be honest. But now there are twenty, thirty news agencies and news websites – all independent, or most of them. But our readership is changing too, we've got a new generation of young readers, under 25 even. They need new products, even here in Kyrgyzstan, maybe especially in Kyrgyzstan do they need this ... not just to read something, also multimedia, news broadcasts.

CHAPTER 8

EVIDENTIAL: HOW ARE MINORITIES COVERED IN THE MEDIA?

This question was again posed in most cases alongside a follow-up question, which was pursued where relevant: What role does (or might) online journalism have in the portrayal of minority linguistic and ethnic groups? The final question revolved around a consideration of the representation of minority linguistic and ethnic groups within both countries. The post-Soviet context is crucial here. Nationalism was supposedly made redundant (on occasion forcibly repressed) under the Soviet system, which was intended to be a free association of many different peoples with Communism fundamentally global in scope. The rationale for including this question was twofold: firstly, independence in the post-Soviet era rendered such "redundant" issues pertinent (indeed, often key political issues) and raised the question of how to negotiate the new paradigm in media terms. Further, it could be argued that the representation of minority groups acts as a kind of litmus test for a free press, in the sense that societies typically move from seeing internal minorities as a threat towards a celebration, or at least tolerance, of diversity. Ahmed (2012) argues that the inability of countries to incorporate minority groups into civic society tends to represent a systemic failure of the state. Online journalism has an obvious potential role to play in this context. For instance, in Malaysia racial and religious issues are highly politicised and the mainstream media has frequently been criticised for its chauvinistic Malay-centric agenda. However, in recent years a subscription-based news website,

139

Malaysiakini, has managed to remain in profit by providing a platform for alternative debate in that country, in particular by articulating the perspectives of minority ethnic groups (Fong and Ishak, 2012).

Clearly, the cultural contexts vary considerably in the post-Colour Revolution environments examined here. Georgia is a classic Caucasian "melting pot" of linguistic groups and ethnicities, as is Kyrgyzstan in the Central Asian context, whereas Ukraine and Armenia are more mono-ethnic in their present forms, although in the case of Armenia this masks a tragic post-Soviet history marked by forms of ethnic cleansing and the forced removal of ethnic and linguistic minorities. However, despite these contextual differences, discussion was allowed to evolve with the result that the debate among Ukrainian journalists revolved around the portrayal (and in some cases media-driven political exploitation) of the supposed "East/West split" in the country, between a Europe-facing, Ukrainian-speaking West, and a Russian-speaking, Russian-facing East. In Armenia, answers revolved around the continuing impasse over the future of Nagorno-Karabakh, an ethnic Armenian enclave in Azerbaijan, at the time of writing still occupied by Armenian troops and unrecognised by the international community. All questions were underpinned by a consideration of the current and potential future role of online journalism in this area: both in terms of the representation of minority groups in the online and mainstream national press, and in terms of the existence or potential of hyperlocal online news provision that represents and articulates their perspectives and concerns.

Because of its ethnic and linguistic diversity, these issues are particularly pertinent in Georgia, where one of the key issues relating to Georgian media freedom is the representation of minorities, which represent 16.2% of the population according to the Georgian Census of 2002 (Yerevan Press Club, 2011). The largest minority communities are Azeri and Armenian, followed by Russians, Abkhazs, Assyrians, Greeks, Jews, Chechens, Kurds, Ossetians and Ukrainians. After the Rose Revolution, the Georgian government implemented several reforms aimed at promoting minority rights, yet there remain criticisms that the government has failed to manage pluralism constructively (Minority Rights Group International, 2009). Article 24(1) of the Georgian constitution guarantees the right to freely receive or impart information, but many of the interviewees claimed that minority communities often face difficulties accessing information in the Georgian media because of the language barrier (Parliament of Georgia, 2012). The public broadcaster is legally bound "to reflect in its programmes ethnic, cultural, linguistic, religious, age and gender diversity of the society and to broadcast programmes in minority languages in proportion" according to Article 16 of Georgia's Law of Broadcasting (2003). But while it does air some programmes, there is only (for instance) one weekly 20-minute news programme in Russian, and the range of print media in minority languages is even more limited.

These issues date back to the disintegration of the Soviet Union and remain particularly pertinent in Caucasian countries like Georgia and Armenia, as well as Kyrgyzstan and other parts of Central Asia, because new nationalist politicians emerged at that time to challenge the Communist elite. Post-Soviet Caucasian and Central Asian nations were therefore particularly susceptible to violent conflict because they were characterised by power struggles on central and sub-national levels. Ethnic groups demanded autonomy, central state structures could not cope and could not contain nationalist developments (Gallina, 2010).

Twenty years on, the Georgian journalists interviewed argued that there are still few ethical standards in the contemporary media when it comes to the reporting of minorities.

> Sofia, Georgia: I would have to say that coverage [of minorities] is either very limited in scope, or, quite often, focused on what you might call "criminal issues". This might involve, er, emphasising a criminal's ethnic or ... even, er ... linguistic group, in the coverage.

A survey by the NGO United Nations Association of Georgia found that the ethnicity of criminals or suspects is regularly emphasised when they are not of Georgian descent (Minority Rights Group International, 2009). Again, this runs counter to the Georgian broadcasting code.

> David, Georgia: Here's what I see as the big issue. If minorities have to rely on their own [foreign] news sources for information, political or otherwise, this is going to make them feel even more isolated within the Georgian state, surely?

The role of the media is, for Siapera (2010), often one of supporting the standardisation that supports the building of the nation-station. This might involve the adoption of a standard language and style of speaking (by the media), alongside a drive towards a standardised education, to homogenise the nation. She argues that nationalism of this kind represents the imposition of a culture that replaces the local folk cultures previously in place. From this point of view, it is not the media content or messages that bind the nation together; rather, the media contribution to the creation and maintenance of the nation can be located in its ability to address the nation in a standard, common language and style. A similar process occurred in many Western European countries in the early years of the twentieth century, with Italy a particularly notable example of a media-driven "national" identity imposed on a much older set of regional identities, replacing – or attempting to replace – linguistic and cultural diversity with a centrally imposed monoculture.

Once ideas of homogeneity and shared identity are established, however, ethno-cultural diversity acquires greater meaning, because it inevitably raises further questions revolving around the question of difference and the "other": who is the dominant group defining itself *against*, in other words. To understand cultural diversity, it is necessary to understand the context that produced it. The post-Soviet histories of the four countries analysed have particular resonance in this context, as they have experienced these processes on several different levels. The Soviet Union itself oscillated between an acceptance and even encouragement of ethnic difference (albeit within the wider context of international Communism) and harsh suppression of linguistic and cultural "difference". Following independence, many states were then forced to confront the reality of their own ethnic mix without the "security" of overarching Soviet identity. Responses and policies varied dramatically: but in many countries, a new form of nationalist and linguistic politics arose echoing the experience of, for instance, the former Yugoslavia. In the post-Soviet world, as in Yugoslavia, opportunistic politicians – often former Communists – tended to resort to nationalist rhetoric in order to create a powerbase in the new political paradigm. This process was particularly notable, and particularly dangerous, in multi-ethnic regions like the Caucasus and Central Asia.

The role of the media is central to this process, in that it supports the standardisation that builds the nation state, in any context: whether "supranational" or newly independent. This form of nationalism may represent the imposition of a culture that seeks to replace or even obliterate the local identities previously in place. Negotiating these complexities in the post-Soviet context was fraught with political difficulty, particularly in the Caucasus and Central Asia, partly because the Soviet era was characterised by a high degree of mobility, but also because these regions have always been characterised by the complexity of their cultural geographies.

Smaller minorities within Georgia and Kyrgyzstan, particularly isolated linguistic groups without external support or a wider linguistic community (for instance, the Abkhaz in Georgia) found themselves in an awkward position post-independence. Global, generalised definitions of the resultant issues are therefore particularly pertinent in the Caucasus and Central Asia, where newly independent states like Georgia and Kyrgyzstan are still involved in the process of nation-building whilst simultaneously tackling the "problem" of accommodating minorities:

> Members of a nation state need to be able to speak the same language in order to communicate and for their bureaucracy to run efficiently; failure to adopt the standardised language and culture then results in problems in communication which must be eradicated. On the other hand, those who do not speak the same, standardised language and who fail to adopt the same cultural practices are seen as hostile to a newly formed

community that has to preserve and transmit its distinctiveness (Siapera, 2010:19).

Gellner talks of a second source of conflict, sometimes relevant in Central Asia and the Caucasus, where "inhibitors" of social entropy are magnified via nationalism and an exclusive approach to nation-building. This process tends to mean that groups possessing certain traits (religion, skin colour) are not assimilated even after several generations. However, despite these barriers, linguistic minorities in Georgia and Kyrgyzstan do recognise the potential of the news media, particularly online, to counteract a lack of representation in the mainstream press. There are numerous examples of Georgian minority groups using the media to develop and discuss political issues.

> Nino M, Georgia: From time to time, they start up their own newspapers. Russians, for example. But their readership is very low ... they are, erm, they're just not encouraged to develop them. There isn't a lot of demand for having a separate (Russian) media as there are still those ... er ... associations with Soviet days, but at the same time there are also programmes broadcast in local minority languages. The public broadcaster has some responsibility in this area and does broadcast occasional programmes in Armenian, for example, but commercial channels don't even consider it.

> David, Georgia: Also the big problem you can see in every field is the lack of, erm, self-governance. For example in regions where Azeri speakers dominate they would, or ... should attempt to have their own media, to organise themselves to have something of their own, something that, um, speaks to them ... but this almost never happens because of social, economic issues. There's just not enough

money for it and most people don't have the information how to ... how to do it. There's an obvious role for the web here I think. It would be cheaper and easier to get something web based off the ground but access rates are very low at the moment. In these regions many people haven't got web access.

The range of Georgian print media available in minority languages is very limited. Although there is little community private funding available, however, there is some governmental financial support provided to *Vrastan*, an Armenian language newspaper, and *Svobodnia Gruzia*, a Russian-language newspaper. However, the latter title focuses largely on entertainment at the expense of politics (Minority Rights Group International, 2009).

> Nino R, Georgia: The government doesn't encourage it either because there is always a threat from ethnic TV because of problems of integration. For example, in the Samtskhe-Javakheti region, in area populated mostly by Armenians it's a very, very touchy issue. After the August 2008 war [in South Ossetia], this region was almost painted by the Georgian media as the *next* separatist region of Georgia, with Armenians depicted as Russia's natural allies. They tried to, er ... organise the people along language lines and it's a very aggressive campaign. For example they have, erm ... numbers ... quotas in higher education for Georgian-speakers who come from Samtskhe-Javakheti. There are two problems I think: a lack of self-governance and a lack of encouragement from the government to strengthen ethnic minority language and culture within the country.

There are localised solutions to some of these issues: for example, there have been attempts to use hyperlocal news media, some of it web based, to articulate the concerns and perspectives of minority ethnic communities within Georgia.

Nana, Georgia: There were two cases in Ninotsminda [where Armenians represent 96% of the population] and [the wider region of] Javakheti (94%), that are populated by ethnic minorities. There were attempts to have community radio stations – this was a huge project financed by BBC World Trust Service in 2006. Two years of the project went by just trying to gain a license, because the regulatory body just refused to grant the license and they were waiting for a response. The only thing they could do was place loudspeakers in the parks, where people would gather to hear news in their own language because they didn't have a license. Then the project was closed down completely.

Gorda, Georgia: Also, you've got to remember that most of these people are not fluent in Georgian. There's a real, um … democratic deficit here. The Russian-speaking community here is very large: Armenians and Azeris generally speak it too … I mean, they speak Russian too [as a lingua franca], but they have may have problems following Russian news, which isn't aimed at them anyway, so they are doubly marginalised and feel more connected with Armenian and Azeri issues.

Nana, Georgia: There is also another really notable development here. There's a newly financed Russian-language channel, with a strong web presence, which you would think would serve the Russian community in Georgia but in reality this channel is directed to the North Caucasus and beyond to feed them good news from Georgia, how good Georgia is, you know. You don't see Russian-speaking Georgians represented on this channel

... their problems, er, how they live. Their interest is just in the Georgian government, how it tackles corruption ... it's basically an attempt to convey a positive message about Georgia.

This refers to the PIK channel, accused of provocation by the Russian authorities. Director General Robert Parsons said at the time of its launch:

It's not our intention to antagonise Moscow. But of course if you have a monopoly over information and somebody arrives on the scene and breaks your monopoly, you're going to find it irritating. And it's our intention to break the Russian government's monopoly over news. We make no secret of that (Georgia Update, 2011).

Georgian Foreign Ministry Deputy Minister Tornike Gordadze sees PIK as part of a larger Georgian policy to reach out to neighbouring groups in Russia: Georgia has to promote its positive image to the North Caucasus to avoid another problem like this, if one day Russia wants to reinvade Georgia, the North Caucasians who are used in the adventure would think twice before following Russia (Brooke, 2011).

When considering the role and political function of minority media within multicultural societies, Habermas's much-quoted emphasis on the role of the media as a public sphere remains the stereotypical starting point: "A realm of our social life in which something approaching public opinion can be formed. Access is guaranteed to all citizens" (Habermas, 1989, p. 49). But the normative function of the media is compromised by economic reality, the pressures of media production and the logic of the market, which all means that the media may not be able to play its politically crucial public sphere role. In this context, true diversity of information and debate is unlikely. Minority media must contribute to the function of the public sphere by providing more and different information, representing different interests and identities (Downing and Husband, 2005, p. 97). The wider question is obvious: how can such forms of news media survive under capitalism? They are unlikely to be competitive in a market situation. One solution is proactive state legislation, or overtly subsidised attempts to circumvent market forces in an effort to protect and sustain linguistic diversity. The 1982 launch of S4C, the Welsh-language channel subsidised by the British government, is an obvious example in a Western context. Another, considerably cheaper, solution is the establishment of web-based news in minority languages although, unlike television, this immediately encounters the access issue, particularly in the post-Soviet areas where it would be most relevant, like the North Caucasus or Southern Kyrgyzstan, which are remote, poor and characterised by limited infrastructural development. Despite this, it provides a potential news platform for minority linguistic communities and holds a "unique promise" for multicultural politics because its interactivity allows for the discussion of contested viewpoints (Downing and Husband, 2005, p. 196).

In Armenia, this line of questioning revolved quite tightly around the relationship with Russia. Despite its proximity to Georgia, Armenia's geopolitical situation and foreign policy is notably different (although it seems likely that Georgia will also attempt to rebalance its relationship with Russia following Saakashvili's defeat in the October 2012 General Election). Russian army bases have long been established along the Armenian–Turkish border, which remained closed at the time of writing in 2012. Armenia walks a foreign policy tightrope, balancing good relations with Russia (on whom it depends for military assistance) and the European Union. The alliance with Russia is partly historic, partly a result of the conflict over the enclave of Nagorno-Karabakh. However, as with many other parts of the former Soviet Union, there is a gradual move away from the use of Russian as lingua franca, particularly among the young: although this remains considerably less noticeable than in Georgia. This is an important context for the Armenian media, which remains dominated by Russian exports as a partial result: this has an inevitable effect on the Armenian public sphere.

> Sonia, Armenia: Most young people now speak English, or at least concentrate on trying to learn it, but it's certainly true that we still all speak Russian. Particularly, I should say, in an ... aural sense. We can all understand it even if a few young people now struggle to express themselves in Russian. So ... sure, we can all understand Russian media, TV news ... and it's often a lot better looking than Armenian TV, if you see what I mean. They have more money, of course. Quite a lot of people, especially the older generation, prefer to watch it (Russian TV) than Armenian TV news, which seems ... er ... cheap by comparison.

In contrast to Georgia, Armenia is relatively mono-ethnic in terms of cultural and linguistic identity. Large-scale in- and out-migration followed the conflict with Azerbaijan over the dispute enclave of Nagorno-Karabakh in the early 1990s. In the Soviet era, for example, Armenia contained several formally established Azerbaijani enclaves. For example, one such enclave, formerly known as Karki (Azeri), now Tigraneshan (Armenian), is located on the present-day Yerevan–Tehran main road. *De jure*, it remains part of Azerbaijan under international law. *De facto*, it is part of Armenia with a small population of Armenian residents who were themselves rehoused there after eviction from Armenian enclaves on the Azeri side of the border. The result of these movements of population is a somewhat mono-ethnic present-day population, although it should be noted that the Armenian journalists questioned occasionally disputed this, and took a generally defensive tone on this issue, pointing to the peaceful coexistence with the largest ethnic minority in Armenia, the Yezidi. However, the Yezidi – a Kurdish-speaking people – are numerically insignificant in Armenia, with no more than 50,000 in the country.

> Sonia, Armenia: Look, there are lots of minorities in Armenia, it's not the mono-ethnic place that people often seem to think. It's just that there's small numbers and, er, I'd have to say there are good relations with all of them ... the Yezidis, Ukrainians, Russians, Kurds.

In terms of the overall geopolitical direction of the subsequent discussion, the distinctive Armenian foreign policy that finely balances relations with both Russia and the West dominated, in much the same way that the East/West cultural split dominated discussion with the Ukrainian participants in this section of the interviews.

> Sonia, Armenia: We balance our relationship between Europe and Russia. Russian troops guard the border with Turkey. I mean they have a military presence here, so we are very different to Georgia, for example. In fact, during the Russian–Georgian war of 2008 we didn't take sides.

The defensiveness in addressing the issue of news media portrayal of minorities, perhaps reflects the fact that this arguably remains a more sensitive issue in Armenia than it is in Georgia, despite the more recent history of conflict in Georgia, largely because of the scale of the conflict over Nagorno-Karabakh and the fact that relations with Azerbaijan continue to dominate Armenian politics. Indeed, intermittent border skirmishes were ongoing at the time of the interviews.

Davit, Armenia: In the world there are no completely independent news sources I think. There are links, there are influences everywhere. Some newspapers here have nationalistic tendencies, yes ... maybe ... but generally minority rights are not violated – though I'd admit sexual minorities are not treated fairly. These [mainstream Armenian] newspapers might compare Armenia with Israel, say, or Georgia, but they never insult Yezidis or Kurds. Yes, they may ... I admit ... insult Turks and Azeris, but not Russians. [When asked to expand this point, he continued]: I myself criticise Azeris and Turks and I've done it in print, but it is not saying "you bloody Azeris" you know? We've got alternative viewpoints too. Russian TV is still influential here, you know, and people go online to check Russian alternative viewpoints. Let's say you were checking news from Syria. People would consult Armenian sources first, then BBC Russia or other Russian sources. Radio Free Europe is also very influential. Some people I know use them as an alternative source, especially the RFE website – they say they don't trust TV and check everything there instead. Remember too that almost all Armenians know or are related to people who have migrated at some point to Russia. So that's important, but people are ... at the same time ... becoming more acquainted with Europe and the US. Previously there was more, er

152

... orientation with Russia. Now, things are more and more balanced.

In the Ukrainian interviews, this initial leading question led in a different direction from the outset with most interviewees focusing on representations of the East/West split in the country. In contrast to the Caucasian ethnic and linguistic diversity exemplified by Georgia, the main cultural and linguistic divide is between Russian-speaking East and a European, Ukrainian-speaking West.

> Maksym, Ukraine: Let's talk about the *Ukrainska Pravda* website again here. Pravda is pan-Ukrainian but ... maybe... let's say it would appeal in Lviv [in the Western Ukrainian heartland] more than Donetsk [in the industrial Russian-speaking East]. I lived in Donetsk for two years and can say that people from Donetsk need, ah, what you might call ... different news ... they're interested in different things. It is still more individualistic in the West, more collective in the East ... where, er, er, they are ... more likely to believe what they're told, shall we say. In the mid 90s there were no journalists in the East, just localised versions of Russian newspapers. In Western Ukraine we have lots of journalists who are popular personalities but journalists are not themselves opinion formers. In the East you do get articles which are anti-Ukrainian, no question, but I would say the West is not anti-Russian except *Svoboda* [a Ukrainian nationalist party] and even they are not anti-Eastern Ukraine. The Russian media thinks Lviv is an anti-Russian centre but this surprises people in Lviv.

Others, however, felt this split was overemphasised and even took exception to such generalisations, again relating them to what they saw as reductive media portrayals and,

153

notably and without prompting, suggesting that online journalism has a role to play in narrowing the gap between East and West Ukraine.

> Vitaly, Ukraine: The divisions in Ukraine are much less noticeable online. In TV debates, some issues are sensitive – language, relations with Russia, the East/West split. But recently I'd say more people consider these issues less important than standards of living and the overall direction Ukraine moves in. There are lots of critical websites in Donetsk, for instance, which show problems in local politics. In fact I'd say Eastern Ukraine has more powerful individual bloggers. People see them as … almost as … an alternative source of information. There are one or two major Donetsk blogs that I know cover crucial issues and news. This East/West gap is much less noticeable online and [has diminished] in the last two years.

This participant, along with some others, strongly refuted what he felt was a politically inspired attempt to over-emphasise the divisions in Ukrainian society and particularly the "division" between Russian East and Ukrainian West. Notably, this respondent and others felt that the reductive media coverage of this issue, and acceptance of the current Ukrainian regime's political "line" on the subject, was a problem in both domestic and foreign media.

> Victor, Ukraine: Many voices across Ukraine are critical of the government online. But TV never shows voices from Donetsk [Eastern, Russian-speaking Ukraine] criticising the government. TV is interested in showing a divided country, whereas the internet, the web world, hates this attempt to divide. I'd say TV is just infotainment in Ukraine, an illusion of democracy, er …

even a kind of manipulation. It seems to be a place of discussion and open debate but there are two main problems. First, you have to make a distinction between real political opposition and opposition funded by government. Why is the opposition funded by the government? Because, um, because the government wants radical opposition like Ukrainian nationalists to deepen the gap between regions and cement its own powerbase in the industrial East.

Ukrainian nationalists like *Svoboda* were making some political headway at the time of the interviews. Seen as imposing values not appealing to Eastern Ukraine, several participants mentioned its "convenience" for the ruling party, which has its powerbase in the Russian-speaking East.

Yevhen, Ukraine: There is no East/West split – it's created by journalists. People can read either language. It's a question of quality. If there was a great idea in journalistic terms that would be popular – it doesn't matter what language or area it's aimed at.

Tetyana, Ukraine: My parents don't buy papers any more. If a website wanted to find a broader audience, bridge the regional divide, we would share loads of values. I definitely think that the East/West differences are overplayed. We're all interested in healthcare for instance. If someone wanted to find common ground they could. And we could, probably ... distance ourselves from the nationalist dimension. The debate just isn't happening – our national TV just has big entertainment shows. *Svoboda* is convenient for the ruling party – it diverts attention away from the immediate issues. It only comes up in local and regional news. *Svoboda* re-emphasises the ... er, rhetoric of the East/

155

West divide. We should try to unite the country around civic values. I sympathise with some of what *Svoboda* says but it is distracting.

M, Ukraine: The West characterises the issues, if they do it at all, badly. It's not about the East/West split ... actually all politicians are basically pro-European. It's not really possible to be a pro-Russian politician. All this is a smokescreen for the main reason they're in Parliament ... to steal money. There's no ideological reason at all. And when it comes to covering all this in the media it's hard, especially for those of us working in print. Lots of people still see journalism as activism.

This participant took a more critical line than most of the other respondents, but represented a more opinionated version of the views expressed by most Ukrainian participants, suggesting that online journalism had an increasing tendency to question what they saw as politically inspired attempts to emphasise the fault lines in Ukrainian culture and society. Similarly, whilst acknowledging the inevitable resource issues, the Georgian journalists all emphasised the real or potential role that online journalism had in articulating the perspectives of minority linguistic and ethnic groups within the country.

In Kyrgyzstan, which has contextual similarities with Georgia in terms of its varied ethnic and linguistic make-up, journalists also independently mentioned the role of online media in this context – albeit with an acknowledgement that infrastructural and economic difficulties meant that its potential was currently not realised. Indeed, one interviewee began by citing traditional clan or family power structures as a key dynamic behind Kyrgyz voting patterns: in this sense, minority communities are able to exert considerable coordinated pressure on central government at certain times.

> C, Kyrgyzstan: In Kyrgyzstan, the older generation that hold political authority still read newspapers. To give you an example, when I went to a wedding in Alai (a region in Southern Kyrgyzstan) I found out that it was the grandfather of the family who decided how the family voted. If someone of that age has a lot of authority, then you are talking about an old man who can influence how entire extended networks of people vote. These *aksakals* (literally "white beard", male elders) get their information from printed word, not the internet. Similarly, the 2010 revolution in Kyrgyzstan was described in some quarters as an Analogue Revolution – the people that put their bodies on the line to remove the President and then looted the city of all it was worth were young men from the regions, not Kloop and Akipress [online news] readers!

The issue of minority representation is arguably more pertinent in Kyrgyzstan than in any other post-Soviet state, including Georgia. The potential for violent inter-ethnic conflict and disputes remains, particularly in the Fergana valley of Southern Kyrgyzstan and neighbouring countries, which is (along with the North Caucasus) perhaps the most unstable and ethnically mixed part of the former Soviet Union. In Southern Kyrgyzstan, there is a significant Uzbek population: representing almost 15% of the overall population of the country, but that figure is far higher in parts of the South. There are four officially recognised Uzbek enclaves and two Tajik enclaves within Kyrgyzstan, and almost eighty ethnic groups live within the country's borders.

The Kyrgyz journalists interviewed in Bishkek were a mixture of ethnic Kyrgyz (four), three ethnic Russians and two with mixed heritage. All Kyrgyz participants responded to this third leading question by first citing media coverage of the ethnic violence in Osh and other Southern regions in 2010, when tensions between ethnic Uzbek and Kyrgyz residents resulted in widespread rioting and hundreds of deaths.

> Elena, Kyrgyzstan: The Kyrgyz become furious about the Osh events, they don't ... they don't want to discuss these issues. Uzbeks say the opposite of course. Really there was guilt on both sides but ... they don't want to accept that. Some discussion takes place online, but a key site (the Fergana site, covered in more depth under question one) was blocked by the government. In the papers ... nothing.

The media's role and responsibility in terms of calming ethnic tensions in Kyrgyzstan is obvious and important, both in terms of the ways in which the national press represents minority groups – Uzbeks in particular – and the ways in which minority communities use the media to engage their own communities in post-conflict dialogue.

> Kuban, Kyrgyzstan: In the South there are Uzbek-language newspapers and an Uzbek TV station, which is ... nationalised, owned by a separatist leader. Information is often disseminated through word of mouth in rural areas, but ... I'd say that people in villages are very often more politicised than urban people, than people in Bishkek. Bishkek people are more passive ... er, definitely voter turnout is lower in the capital. Politics is actually ... ah, *done* in the provinces. Political turmoil originates in the provinces and ends up here. The unrest in 2005 for instance, took place first in the regions. And in 2010 it all started in Jalalabad. So, to an extent, access to the media doesn't affect the degree of politicisation. Having said that,

my experience is that our regions are ... more hungry for information, they're very keen. What's maybe, er, surprising is that our provinces are interested in national issues maybe more than local. It's become a habit to protest in the capital. For example there was a political rally here very recently, a few days ago ... they wanted three specific MPs out. At other times, ethnic issues become very ... hot, and destabilising in the media.

Begaim, Kyrgyzstan: Fans of wars and ... let's say ... compromising evidences [the author took this to mean "conspiracy theories"] can find enough information online to discuss endlessly. We have very small expert community who all know each other, but on the other hand I do think the internet here in Kyrgyzstan has real political influence, and this influence will grow further. Due to the fact that the main state structures work in the capital city, everything that appears online, er ... immediately receives a ... reaction from government agencies.

All the ethnic Russian journalists, and two of the ethnic Kyrgyz journalists, suggested that Kyrgyz-language newspapers – whether based in the capital Bishkek or in the South – played some kind of role (albeit indirect) in destabilising the political situation in the country, in the sense that their portrayal of the Uzbek minority, in particular, was sometimes inflammatory. A contrast was drawn with Russian-language papers, which tend to be based in the (Russian-speaking) capital, Bishkek. The first view here is from an ethnic Kyrgyz journalist: the second from an ethnic Russian born and bred in Bishkek.

Kuban, Kyrgyzstan: I'd say Russian [language] papers are a bit more professional, less focused on "yellow" stuff, rumours that sometimes lead to ... violence even if not directly.

Shades of Expression

Elena, Kyrgyzstan: Many Russians have left over the years, journalists included of course. One Russian paper has unofficial protection from the Russian embassy, you know ... and it covers many crimes happening here. Kyrgyz journalists are less educated in my view, they're less familiar with international standards. They have an ... Asian mentality based on, er ... informal relationships. They have their own networks and what they write is often ... usually ... yellow journalism. One may provide information from his friend ... "I know him, he says this, so it must be true". It's really a huge problem. The most recent Presidential election was covered completely differently by the Kyrgyz and Russian press, you know. We need to educate Kyrgyz-language journalists. At the moment it's really one-sided, with many issues connected to nationalism, anti-Uzbek content ... and some anti-Russian sentiment, you know? And there's no real legislation to control it all.

This was perhaps the most contentious of all the opinions expressed on this issue, and the participant was asked to further elaborate and, in particular, to clarify the latter claim.

Elena, Kyrgyzstan: Our constitution guarantees freedom of the press but the reality is that the system doesn't work. They cancelled the defamation law, to support freedom of the press ... yes, that is true. But there are deeper ... bigger problems, and that, er, cancellation will lead to bigger problems itself. When it comes to ... minorities, language groups, ethnic peoples, they don't have much of a ... say. There are Uzbek papers in the South, where there are lots of other communities, like Tajiks, trying to promote cultural values and using the media to a small extent to do this. The government is trying to promote an effective minority policy, because it has been and will remain a

160

major problem, but there's no official status for the Uzbek language, for example.

A rather more measured view came from a Kyrgyz participant with a somewhat broader perspective on these issues. He also cited a gap in "quality" between the Russian and Kyrgyz-language press, but independently cited the potential for online journalism to act as at least a partial solution to the narrow issue of media representation of minority groups – if not the wider ethnic tensions within Southern Kyrgyzstan.

C, Kyrgyzstan: At any rate the paper press is often not responsible. The online press tends to be better, and the gulf in quality … which I'd say is particularly, er, notice-able between Russian-language online content and Kyrgyz-language newspapers, can be seen at Gezitter.org. Gezitter translates the Kyrgyz press into Russian. Some of the articles there are little more than vicious gossip. However, as far as I am aware, open ethnic slurs against Uzbeks and other groups in the printed press have decreased since late 2010 so this is a positive trend that suggests a degree of responsibility is appearing.

CHAPTER 9

CONCLUSION: THE DEMOCRATISING POTENTIAL OF INDEPENDENT "HUB" WEBSITES

The evolution of "Western" analyses of the democratising potential of online media has gone through several distinct phases. Discussion initially revolved around whether new media could be trusted, and then evolved to consider whether new media threatened journalistic professionalism. It gradually moved on to considerations of whether it would destroy the mainstream press itself. Then came a gradual acceptance that blogs (to take one example) were simply an adjunct to the mainstream press, adding diversity but arguably lacking real impact. Such conclusions tend to be framed in terms of technology-generated journalistic "convergence". Bivens (2008), for example, found that mainstream UK and Canadian journalism's adaptations to new media were resulting in largely beneficial shifts to traditional news flow cycles and even news values, as well as heightened accountability.

However, the results of the interviews conducted for this book suggests that such debates should perhaps be confined to Western contexts as they inevitably tend to be framed from the perspective of established, mainstream news organisations – because this is where "convergence" becomes most significant in its effects in countries like Canada and the UK. In contrast, the role of online journalism in its broadest sense is considerably more politically significant in more deficient media environments, particularly those lacking a long-established tradition of independent print journalism. In these contexts, "convergence" is a less relevant concept. Further, the work

162

argues that the clearest indication of this significance is currently seen in the "semi-free" journalistic environments of "West-facing" parts of the former Soviet Union, particularly those countries like Georgia, Kyrgyzstan and Ukraine that experienced Colour Revolutions in the mid 2000s, where demands for a free press played a central role and where the news media's real and potential political impact continues to underpin political debate in a way rarely seen in the West. This is intrinsically linked to the post-Colour Revolution experience of all four countries, which illustrates the complex nature of social processes, political participation, inter-ethnic dynamics and political development in the post-Soviet space (Marat, 2006).

In these environments, there are signs of a coalescing around what the author argues can be best described as "news hub" or portal websites: indeed, this is the key finding to emerge from the fieldwork. Such sites are not blogs: they echo but transcend the blogging format. Neither are they established news organisations trialling methods of mobilising and hosting new media for commercial reasons, which often characterises high-profile news portals in the West (cf. Bivens, 2008, Braun and Gillespie, 2011). Indeed, this is a crucial distinction. They are, rather, independently funded sources of exclusively online political journalism that have identified and *deliberately address* shortcomings in the mainstream news media. Websites such as *Netgazeti* and *Liberali* in Georgia, and *Ukrainska Pravda* in Ukraine, are a genuinely alternative media response to topical political issues and echo similar examples in entirely different media contexts (for instance, *WalesHome*, which formerly addressed a structurally deficient media environment in post-devolution Wales, and *Nawaat.org* which functions as a post-"Arab Spring" hub for Tunisian political journalism). They are all concerted and overtly journalistic attempts to circumvent the mainstream press and often do the job of conveying political information more effectively than conventional journalism in these environments. Further, they act as a filtering system for the mass of information deriving from social media like Twitter and Facebook, as well as conveying and collating the perspectives of individual bloggers. They have, in other words, assumed an editorial or gatekeeping role, channelling online opinion through professional journalistic techniques and giving rise to new (but edited) forms of self-expression. Funding models for such sites are complex as they often find it difficult to attract advertisers, who may shy away from controversial content in such environments. However, there are signs of independent and robust funding models emerging. For instance, *Malaysiakini,* another hub website that deliberately seeks to provide an alternative to the mainstream press in Malaysia (a country in which racial and religious issues are highly politicised), is a subscription-based website that makes a profit, derived from small numbers of committed readers who recognise its value in providing alternative journalistic perspectives (Fong and Ishak, 2012). Post-Soviet sites such as *Netgazeti* and *Ukrainska Pravda* continue to depend at least partially on small grants from foreign donors and NGOs, in combination with income from advertisers and commercial backers.

Beckett (2008) argues that the distinction between weblogs and traditional media is becoming increasingly blurred as journalism goes online, while Roberts (2011) suggests that, in many different contexts characterised by a structurally deficient mainstream media, an advanced, hybrid form of web-based journalism is developing, a form that begins to set a wider media agenda without necessarily referencing or involving the traditional press. Applying Messner and DiStasto's "source cycle" (2008) model to the post-Colour Revolution countries is, in short, almost impossible. Journalists in all four countries argued that web-based news frequently supplanted or sidestepped the mainstream media, whereas Messner and DiStasto found a mutually beneficial relationship between blogs and the mainstream press in the US context: blogs create a "buzz" about an issue or story, the mainstream press pick it up, then online media recycles, analyses and reinterprets the original story as it evolves. In the US context, online media is therefore defined in terms of its relationship with the mainstream press: its influence is measured by its impact on the mainstream press. The post-Soviet experience is very different, and has to be viewed in the context of the earlier Colour Revolutions: with the news media's real and potential democratic impact still a live and important part of political debate. The fact that this debate and the related evolution of wider democratic systems in the post-Colour Revolution nations is coinciding with the rapid evolution of web-based technology increases the impact of news websites that seek to advance and extend the public sphere in such environments.

Writing in the Western context, Beckett (2008) suggests that, instead of the old polarity, it is more useful to think in terms of personal bloggers and journalist bloggers who are both effectively "networked journalists". In the smaller-scale media environments typical of post-Soviet independent states, such networks are able to leverage greater impact. Numbers accessing hub news sites in the four countries analysed may be relatively low, but their influence on the mainstream press and wider political agenda is magnified by that small scale, and, echoing Megenta (2011) in the context of authoritarian African regimes, those numbers are not necessarily the most relevant issue. Rather, it is a question of influence, of who and what those engaged readers represent. To further illustrate this point, China is often cited in discussions about the democratising potential of new media, and serves to echo Megenta's argument in a very different socio-economic context, in the sense that a small minority of politically engaged web users are using online technology to develop new public spheres in China. Scotton and Hachten (2010) suggest that Chinese authorities are simply overwhelmed by the use of new media by young people and their ability to use it to link to others both in China and elsewhere, often to raise questions about the existing regime. New media in China are, they argue, at the frontier of the media changes that are bringing a new openness to the country. The web is becoming a prominent political instrument, though authorities see uncontrolled access as a serious threat and have undertaken stringent controls to contain it. This echoes the experience in the more authoritarian regimes in the former Soviet Union: those countries that have often adopted a very different approach to the management of news and information to the post-Colour Revolution nations examined in this book. The problems inherent in such media environments place the evolving media strategies of the post-Colour Revolution nations in sharper focus. Writing in the post-Soviet, but *pre*-Colour Revolution context, Sparks (2000) made a plea for debates surrounding media and democracy to move away from the virtues of "state versus market" and turn to relations between the media and the public, arguing that democratising the media means breaking the control of those elites over what are necessarily the main means of public speech in large-scale societies. Over a decade later, in countries such as Azerbaijan, Belarus and Uzbekistan, strict controls over web-based news mean that the public sphere role of online journalism – and the media in general – remains hugely restricted.

In such contexts, defining the differences between citizen journalism, public journalism, civic, participatory and community journalism may be important: in that "Arab Spring" style attempts to circumvent oppressive media restrictions via various forms of online self-expression often characterise web use in such environments. Erjavec and Kovacic (2008) points out that such gradations are not precisely or unanimously defined in mass communication literature. But whereas such definitions may be important in authoritarian contexts like Uzbekistan, or parts of sub-Saharan Africa, where small numbers of online activists operate in direct opposition to the authorities, the Post-Colour Revolution environments examined in this book do not lend themselves to such a precise use of definitional language. Indeed, it would be inappropriate, because the hub websites characterising contemporary news journalism in Ukraine, Georgia, Kyrgyzstan and Armenia are notable for the fact that they transcend such precise definitions by marshalling a range of journalistic material online. If the primary communicative purpose in citizen journalism relates to an approach that addresses people as citizens and potential participants in public affairs, helps the political community to act upon its problems, and improves the climate of public discussion (Rosen, 1999) then precise definitions in such contexts are irrelevant. The concept of an active audience, which contributes to public life, engaged by a media which searches for solutions not just the presentation of problems, may contrast sharply with journalistic practices in Western contexts, and increasingly with public perceptions of journalists' roles in those contexts. However, such idealistic concepts continue to characterise the wider view of journalists' role in the post-Colour Revolution context.

Indeed, Hanitzsch et al. (2011) found several similarities between contemporary journalistic cultures in varied contexts worldwide, in particular the global primacy of role perceptions that are characterised by detachment and non-involvement. Acting as government watchdog also seemed a universal aspiration, alongside a consensus regarding the adherence to universal principles to be followed regardless of context. For O'Neill (2012) a genuinely free press requires that media communication is "assessable", with audiences getting the information they need about the evidence, the interested parties and the funding behind it. The triangular relationship between the state, the citizen and the public sphere remains at the heart of all such debates about the value and role of journalism. Habermas's contested views on the public sphere arguably remain core to media theory and inevitably remain relevant in the context of the "Arab Spring" – notwithstanding the cautionary writings of Schudson (2008) who points out that journalism has long existed outside democracy and that journalism does not by itself produce or provide democracy. Indeed, several writers are critical of the tendency to cite Habermas's notion of the public sphere without reference to the contextual specificity: the emerging middle class in seventeenth and eighteenth century Western Europe (Louw, 2010, for instance). It remains a useful shorthand, however, as, in most idealistic interpretations part of journalism's purpose is to encourage civic participation, improve public debate and enhance public life without sacrificing the independence of a free press. For Habermas (1989), that brief moment in time represented a period when political action was driven by "authentic public opinion" as opposed to manufactured and/or manipulated public opinion.

Addressing the relationship between journalism and citizenship in relation to post-web technological change, Papacharissi (2009) argues that journalism enables and amplifies conversations of varying content as it evolves to cater to an audience equipped with the ability to consume and produce its own media content. The challenge is for a style of journalism that best serves the typical "monitorial" citizen of our contemporary "networked" post-web societies. Stepping back from public spaces, citizens can choose to engage or disengage from their civic duties as they choose: but they do so largely from private spheres of web-enabled activity. Globally, there are much earlier precedents for the notion of countering perceived deficiencies in the mainstream media by attempting to exploit the interactivity offered by web-based technology. Arguably the most famous was the 1999 launch of OhMyNews in South Korea with the tagline: "Every citizen is a journalist". Founder Oh Yeon-Ho expressed his frustration with the "haughty attitude common in the Korean media" by involving more than 700 "citizen reporters" in his attempt to circumvent the mainstream Korean press and supply news from their own perspectives.

The words of Ruslan, one of the Ukrainian interviews, seem pertinent in this context, as he articulates the pseudo-Habermasian idealism inherent in the kind of hyperlocal web-based journalism now gaining a foothold in parts of provincial Ukraine.

Traditional papers are not doing well in Ukrainian regions – even in small cities people are moving to the web for news. Print media tend to be oblast owned, same as they were in the Soviet era, with small print runs. So the pan-Ukrainian sites like *Pravda* take over as a news source. But it's not just that: there are also successful local examples – in Sumi an interesting project substitutes existing old media with a news website. It tells local people what they need to know – about schools, shops, jobs, you know. Journalists everywhere are doing hyper-local political journalism. Local (mainstream) journalists used to write about the local Communist party so they still think this is what their audience wants. There's no tradition to write about real local issues. Journalists talk about local politicians at the expense of, say, potholes in the road. People are tired of political talkshows, disappointed in traditional media and its capacity to explain the world around them. It's detached from reality hence the popularity of social networks and hence the popularity and importance of these local websites and of *Ukrainska Pravda*. Online, journalists can write and say what they think and write things they can't do in their [mainstream] articles (Ruslan, personal communication, 8 February 2012).

Such comments are notably optimistic and perhaps geopolitically specific. A more cautious approach has characterised general debate about the effect of web-based journalism on the public sphere. Markham (2010) for example, argues that if the democratising effect of the "blogosphere" is judged by the level of interaction it generates, this needs to be balanced against the argument that interaction is not in any sense democratising unless it leads to some form of action or deliberation, and that while different groups may benefit from a new configuration of power relations based on interactivity, there is no reason to invest the shift itself with a teleology of democratising reform. In certain post-Soviet contexts, however, it could be argued that such a critique is rather less pertinent, partly because of the radically different mainstream media and political environment, but also because the news hub websites cited by the participants directly address deficiencies in the mainstream media and therefore position themselves differently at the outset. While political blogs and online "hubs" are certainly not always immune from self-referential navel-gazing and are often partisan, the sites considered here are subject to wider legislative and editorial constraints. They bring a version of independent journalistic professionalism to bear in environments that have a limited tradition of this. This is particularly true if we consider online political journalism in its broadest sense, in which some sites specifically intend to provide a space for the kind of debate that is lacking in the mainstream press and therefore deliberately place more emphasis on objectivity, analysis and interactivity. The responses of the interviewees strongly suggests that they are beginning to have some meaningful impact on the political sphere in Ukraine, Georgia, Armenia and Kyrgyzstan. The value of qualitative analysis, as opposed to the aggregation of page impressions, is arguably to reveal the real cultural purchase of online journalism in these contexts. It becomes apparent through wider debate among what Megenta (2011) calls the "non-regime elites".

Megenta (2011), writing in the context of authoritarian regimes in Africa, argues that analysts ought not to predict the impact of internet-enabled news on democratic change solely based on the number of people who use it. The internet's effect on politics in some countries with very low connectivity has been noteworthy, he suggests, because its users are mostly members of social groups that have significant political influence. Early adopters have significant roles in setting the direction for the technology's future use in those environments. Ukraine, Georgia and Armenia have relatively high rates of web access, but are similarly impoverished in terms of, for instance, the conventional print media. Therefore, the political impact of online journalism is magnified considerably. Those accessing "hub" news sites in the post-Colour Revolution nations do so from an elevated position in terms of existing knowledge: their perspective tends to be international in scope, but their numbers are far higher than in sub-Saharan Africa. The best comparison is arguably with contemporary Tunisia, where much higher penetration rates meant that hub websites like *nawaat.org* "immediately became an alternative and subversive public sphere of participation and challenge to information dominance" (Megenta, 2011, p. 96). Tunisians were politicised by providing them with spaces of political participation in which a combination of professional journalists and interested citizens were able to expose corruption and abuses by the government. Whilst the political situation in the post-Colour Revolution nations does not bear direct comparison, there are similarities in terms of the rapid evolution of the wider political system, and the general point stands: the audience for web-based news is younger and, almost by definition, politically active and dissatisfied with the ruling regime and the mainstream media. Their influence is then magnified by the networked nature of hub news websites. For optimists, the democratic potential of the web can be genuinely harnessed by these forms, which may not herald the end of the mainstream news monopoly on information in the West, but can at least enrich the public sphere in contexts where the mainstream press is less developed.

Further to this, it should be noted that some of the traditional scepticism about blogging and online journalism in the academic and journalistic communities is beginning to be questioned by those with a different perspective on these issues. These criticisms are worthy of note, as they question the validity of academic caution in relation to the rapid evolution of the online environment. *The Guardian's* web editor Emily Bell, for instance, ended a recent review with the following critique of research into online journalism:

> Unlinked and frozen in time, its weighty discourse is undermined by its immutable nature. Some of the bigger themes of normative news agendas and democratic purpose are truly worthy of expansion, while some of the more micro observations about journalism and politics already seem dated and dispensable (Bell, 2010).

Journalism is tasked with examining the present, the issues of the day: but the delays associated with academic publishing mean they tend to focus on broader theoretical and conceptual issues and lack the urgency and vitality of more "journalistic" books (Keeble, 2012). Boler (2008) developed this critique further, noting that one of the greatest challenges of conducting media studies at this historical moment is to keep apace with the rapidly changing face of media use, production and practices, both corporate and independent. In the context of media and political environments like the post-Colour Revolution nations, such criticisms are highly pertinent, cautioning against an overly pessimistic assessment of the democratising potential of online forms of journalism, whilst simultaneously illustrating the difficulty of applying cogent academic analysis to a rapidly evolving, highly politicised media milieu. Providing a snapshot of that evolution is perhaps the most meaningful solution – in the sense that an exploration of that "moment in time" might have wider resonance in terms of the longer term democratising potential of online news media as technology itself evolves in conjunction with democratic systems in the post-Colour Revolution nations.

REFERENCES

Abbasov, S., & Grigoryan, M. (2012). *Georgia: Is Tbilisi setting political benchmark for Azerbaijan, Armenia?* Retrieved from: http://www.eurasianet.org/node/66027.

Agre, P. (2002). Real-time Politics: The internet and the political process. *The Information Society, 18*, 311–31.

Ahmed, A. (2012). *Putin's Challenge: The Circassians and the Winter Olympics.* Retrieved from: http://www.aljazeera.com/indepth/opinion/2012/04/2012446515233997.html

Allan, S., & Thorsen, E. (2009). *Citizen Journalism: Global perspectives.* Oxford, United Kingdom: Peter Lang Publishing.

Anderson, J. (1999). *Kyrgyzstan: Central Asia's island of democracy?* London, United Kingdom: Routledge.

Archetti, C. (2012). Which future for foreign correspondence? *Journalism Studies. 13*(5–6), 847–56.

Atton, C., & Hamilton, J. (2011). *Alternative Journalism.* London, United Kingdom: Sage.

Beckett, C. (2008). *Supermedia: Saving journalism so it can save the world.* London, United Kingdom: Wiley-Blackwell.

Beckett, C. (2010). *The Value of Networked Journalism.* London, United Kingdom: LSE/Polis.

Bell, E. (2010). [Review of the book *New Media, Old News*]. *British Journalism Review, 21*(1), 83.

Berger, G. (2009). How the internet impacts on international news: Exploring paradoxes of the most global medium in a time of "hyperlocalism". *The International Communication Gazette, 71*,(5), 366–76.

Bivens, R. (2008). The internet, mobile phones and blogging. *Journalism Practice, 2*(1), 113–129.

Blumler, J., & Gurevitch, M. (1995). *The Crisis of Public Communication.* Hove, United Kingdom: Psychology Press.

Blumler, J., & Coleman, S. (2001). *Realising Democracy Online: A civic commons in cyberspace.* London, United Kingdom: Institute of Public Policy Research.

Blumler, J. (2012). A journey to and through the political communication research terrain. Retrieved from: http://pasamediaandpoliticsgroup.worldpress.com

Boler, M. (2008). *Digital Media and Democracy: Tactics in hard times.* Cambridge, MA: MIT Press.

Braun, J. & Gillespie, T. (2011). Hosting the public discourse, hosting the public. *Journalism Practice*, 5(4), 383–98.

Brooke, J. (2011, August 11). Georgian TV beams Russian language news to Russia. Retrieved from http://www.voanews.com/content/georgian-tv-beams -russian-language-news-to-russia-127616033/143748. html

Burrett, T. (2012, October 1). Orange squash: Foul play in Ukraine. *New Internationalist.*

Caryl, C. (2012). *The Georgian Paradox,* Retrieved from: www.foreignpolicy.com

Chaulia, S. (2006). Democratisation, NGOs and "Colour Revolutions". Retrieved from http://www. opendemocracy.net/globalization-institutions_ govern ment/colour_revolutions_3196.jsp

Cheterian, V. (2011). The Arab revolt and the Colour Revolutions. Retrieved from http://www. opendemocracy.net/vicken-cheterian/arab-revolt-and- colour-revolutions

Clarke, H. & Schober, M. (1992). Asking questions and influencing answers. In J. Tanner (Ed.), *Questions About*

Questions: Inquiries into the cognitive bases of surveys. New York, NY: Russell Sage Foundation.

Coleman, S. & Blumler, J. (2009). *The Internet and Democratic Citizenship.* Cambridge, United Kingdom: Cambridge University Press.

Columbia Journalism Review. (2012, September/October). Special Report: The future of media.

Companjen, F. (2010). Georgia. In D. O'Beachain, & A. Polese (Eds.), *The Colour Revolutions in the Former Soviet Republics: Successes and failures* (pp. 13–30). Abingdon, United Kingdom: Routledge.

Copsey, N. (2010). Ukraine. In D. O'Beachain, & A. Polese (Eds.), *The Colour Revolutions in the Former Soviet Republics: Successes and failures* (pp. 30–45). Abingdon, United Kingdom: Routledge.

Curran, J. & Park, M.-J. (2000). *De-Westernizing Media Studies.* Abingdon, United Kingdom: Routledge.

Cushion, S., Lewis, J., & Groves, C. (2009). Reflecting the Four Nations? An analysis of reporting devolution on UK network news media. *Journalism Studies, 10*(5), 1–17.

Dahlgren, P. (2005). The internet, public spheres and political communication: Dispersion and deliberation. *Political Communication, 22*(2), 147–62.

Davies, G. (2009). *Media in Wales: Serving public values?* Cardiff, United Kingdom: Institute of Welsh Affairs.

De Waal, T. (2010). *The Caucasus.* Oxford, United Kingdom: Oxford University Press.

Deibert, R., Haraszti, M., Palfrey, J., Rohozinski, R., & Zittrain, J. (2010). Access Controlled: The shaping of power, rights, and rule in cyberspace. Cambridge, MA: MIT Press.

Downing, J. & Husband, C. (2005). *Representing 'Race':*
Racisms, ethnicities and the media. London, United
Kingdom: Sage.

Drezner, D., & Farrell, H. (2004). *The Power and Politics of*
Blogs. Retrieved from http://www.yale.edu/
lawweb/jbalkin/telecom/dreznerandfarrellblogpaper
final.pdf

The Economist (2012a, October 6). A stunning victory.

The Economist (2012b, May 7). No half time oranges for
Victor.

The Economist (2012c, May 7). Sargsyan sees.

The Economist (2012d, September 8). The axeman goeth.

Erjavec, K. & Kovacic, M. (2008). Mobi journalism in
Slovenia. *Journalism Studies,* 9(6), 874–90.

European Commisssion (2009). Eastern Partnership.
Retrieved from http://ec.europa.eu/europeaid/where/
neighbourhood/regional-cooperation/enpi-east/index_
en.htm

European Commission (2012). *External Relations.* Retrieved
from: http://www.eeas.europa.eu/index_en.htm

Fergananews (2012). Experts condemn blocking Fergana's
website as illegal and senseless. Retrieved from
http://enews.fergananews.com/articles/2746

Fielden, L. (2012). *Regulating the Press: A comparative study of*
international press councils. Oxford, United Kingdom:
Reuters Institute for the Study of Journalism/University
of Oxford.

Filiu, J.-P. (2011). *The Arab Revolution: Ten lessons from the*
democratic uprising. London, United Kingdom: C. Hurst
& Co.

Fong, Y. L., & Ishak, S. A. (2012, December). *The role of*
mainstream and alternative newspapers in promoting racial
integration in Malaysia. Paper presented at the 1st Annual

References

International Conference on Journalism and Mass Communications, Singapore.

Fossato, F. & Lloyd, J. (2008). *The Web that Failed: How opposition politics and independent initiatives are failing on the internet in Russia.* Oxford, United Kingdom: Reuters Institute for the Study of Journalism/University of Oxford.

Frake, C. (1977). Plying frames can be dangerous. *Quarterly Newsletter of the Institute for Comparative Human Development.* 1(3) 1–7.

Franklin, B. (1997). *Newszak and News Media.* London, United Kingdom: Hodder Arnold.

Freedom House (2011). *Freedom of the Press Report.* Retrieved from http://www.freedomhouse.org/report

Freedom House (2012). *Nations in Transit: Fragile frontier.* Retrieved from: http://www.freedomhouse.org/sites/default/files/Release%20Booklet.pdf

Fumagalli, M. & Tordjman, S. (2010). Uzbekistan. In D. O'Beachain & A. Polese (Eds.), *The Colour Revolutions in the Former Soviet Republics: Successes and Failures* (pp. 156–77). Abingdon, United Kingdom: Routledge.

Gallina, N. (2010). Puzzles of state transformation: The cases of Armenia and Georgia. *Caucasian Review of International Affairs, 4* (1), Winter.

Galtung, J. (1990). Theory formation in social research: a plea for pluralism. In E. Oyen (Ed.), *Comparative Methodology: Theory and practice in international social research* (pp. 101–10). London, United Kingdom: Sage.

Garton Ash, T. (2004) *Free World: Why a crisis of the West reveals the opportunity of our time.* London, United Kingdom: Penguin.

Geniets, A. (2011). *Trust in International News Media in Partially Free Media Environments.* Oxford: Reuters

Institute for the Study of Journalism/University of Oxford.

Georgian Law of Broadcasting (2003). Retrieved from www.wipo.int

Georgia Update (2011, February 3). Retrieved from www.georgiaupdate.gov.ge

Gilmor, D. (2004). *We the Media: Grassroots Journalism by the people, for the people.* New York, NY: O'Reilly.

Greenall, R. (2012). *LiveJournal: Russia's unlikely internet giant.* Retrieved from: www.bbc.co.uk/news/magazine-17177053

Haas, T. (2005). From "public journalism" to the "public's journalism"? Rhetoric and reality in the discourse on weblogs. *Journalism Studies, 6,* 387–96.

Habermas, J. (1989). *The Structural Transformation of the Public Sphere: An inquiry into a category of bourgeois society.* Cambridge, MA: MIT Press.

Hachten, W., & Scotton, J. (2011). *The World News Prism: Global information in a satellite age.* Oxford, United Kingdom: Blackwell Publishing.

Hale, H. (2005). Regime Cycles: Democracy, autocracy and revolution in Post-Soviet Eurasia. *World Politics, 58*(1), 133–65.

Hallin, D. & Mancini, P. (2004). *Comparing Media Systems: Three models of media and politics.* New York, NY: Cambridge University Press.

Hanitzsch, T. (2008). Comparing journalism across cultural boundaries. In M. Loffelholz & D. Weaver (Eds.), *Global Journalism Research: Theories, methods, findings, future* (pp. 93–105) Malden, MA: Blackwell.

Hanitzsch, T. et al. (2011). Mapping Journalism Cultures across Nations. *Journalism Studies, 12*(3), 273–93.

References

Harding, L. (2012, October 2). Georgia's President Saakashvili concedes election defeat. *The Guardian*, p. 7.

Hofstede, G. (2001). *Culture's Consequences: Comparing values, behaviors, institutions and organizations across nations.* Thousand Oaks, CA: Sage.

Huntington, S. (1991). *The Third Wave: Democratisation in the late 20th century.* Oklahoma, OK: University of Oklahoma Press.

Internews (2012). Retrieved from https://innovation.internews.org/blogs/armenian-elections-monitoring-crowdsourcing-public-journalism-mapping

Iskandaryan, A. (2005). *Armenia: What the election showed.* Yerevan, Armenia: CMI.

Ismailov, A. (2011). *Kyrgyzstan: Government bans news websites from the election campaign.* Retrieved from http://globalvoicesonline.org

Jakubowitz, K. (2001). *Rude Awakening: Social and media change in Central and Eastern Europe.* New York, NY: Hampton Press.

Keeble, R. (2012). A new model for academic publishing? *Three-D MeCCSA Newsletter* (19).

Khiabany, G. & Srebeny, A. (2009). The Iranian story: What citizens? What journalism? In S. Allan & E. Thorsen (Eds.), *Citizen Journalism: Global perspectives.* New York, NY: Peter Lang Publishing.

Kilner, J. (2012, June 17). Kyrgyzstan is a beacon of democracy in autocratic Central Asia says ex-leader. *Daily Telegraph.*

Kostanyan, H. & Tsertsvadze, T. (2012). *The Fading Rose of Georgia's Revolution: Will elections bring fresh hope?* Brussels, Belgium: Centre for European Policy Studies.

181

Kumkova, K. (2012, October 18). *Kyrgyzstan: Language and media still sensitive subjects in southern regions.* Retrieved from: http://www.eurasianet.org/node/66068

Kung, L., Picard, R., & Towse, R. (2008). *The Internet and the Mass Media.* London, United Kingdom: Sage.

Lasas, A. (2013, February). *Trust dividend of transition: The dynamics of political and media trust in the European Union.* Paper presented at the Audiences, Media Environments and Democratization after the Arab Spring Conference, University of Oxford/Reuters Institute for the Study of Journalism.

Lasica, J. (2003). Blogs and journalism need each other. *Nieman Reports,* Fall 2003, 70–75.

Lee, L. (2012, September 13) Kyrgyzstan's new government faces serious challenges. *Times of Central Asia.*

Lewis, D. (2010). Kyrgyzstan. In D. O'Beachain, & A. Polese (Eds.), *The Colour Revolutions in the Former Soviet Republics: Successes and failures.* Abingdon, United Kingdom: Routledge.

Lievrouw, L. (2011). *Alternative and Activist New Media.* Cambridge, United Kingdom: Polity Press.

Livingstone, S. (2003). On the challenges of cross-national comparative media research. *European Journal of Communication, 18*(4), 477–500.

Locke, J. (1966). *The Second Treatise of Government.* Oxford, United Kingdom: Basil Blackwell.

Louw, E. (2010). *The Media and Political Process.* London, United Kingdom: Sage.

Manzella, J., & Yacher, L. (2005). The Kyrgyz Republic's liminal media: Assessing a journalistic rite of passage. *Journalism Studies, 6*(4), 431–43.

Marat, E. (2006). *The Tulip Revolution: One year after.* Washington, DC: The Jamestown Foundation.

References

Markham, T. (2010). The case against the democratic influence of the internet on journalism. In G. Monaghan & S. Tunney (Eds.), *Web Journalism: A new form of citizenship?* (pp. 77–97). Eastbourne, Sussex: Sussex Academic Press.

Markham, T. (2013, February). *Media and political subjectivity in the Arab Spring: Projection, experience, deliberation.* Paper presented at the Audiences, Media Environments and Democratization after the Arab Spring Conference, University of Oxford/Reuters Institute for the Study of Journalism.

Mashrab, F. (2012, September 21). Bishkek hands Putin Kyrgyz independence. *Asia Times.*

Mason, P. (2012). *Why it's Kicking Off Everywhere: The new global revolutions.* London, United Kingdom: Verso.

Mason, P. (2013). *Why it's Still Kicking Off Everywhere: The new global revolutions.* London, United Kingdom: Verso.

Matheson, D. (2009). What the Blogger Knows. In Z. Papacharissi (Ed.), *Journalism and Citizenship: New Agendas in Communication.* Abingdon, United Kingdom: Routledge.

McLaughlin, D. (2012, November 10). Georgian PM accused of witch-hunt after high-profile arrests. *Irish Times.*

McNair, B. (2000). *Journalism and Democracy: An evaluation of the political public sphere.* London, United Kingdom: Routledge.

McNair, B. (2001). Media professionals in the former Soviet Union. In J. Tunstall (Ed.), *Media Occupations and Professions.* Oxford, United Kingdom: Oxford University Press.

Megenta, A. (2011). *Can it Tweet its Way to Democracy? The promise of participatory media in Africa.* Oxford, United Kingdom: Reuters Institute for the Study of Journalism.

Messner, M., & DiStasto, M. (2008). The source cycle: How traditional media and weblogs use each other as sources, *Journalism Studies, 9*(3), 447–63.

Minority Rights Group International (2009) *Breaking the Cycle of Exclusion: Minority rights in Georgia today.* London, United Kingdom: Minority Rights Group International.

Mitchell, L. (2012). *The Color Revolutions.* Philadelphia, PA: University of Pennsylvania Press.

Morley, D. (1980). *The 'Nationwide' Audience: Structure and decoding,* London, United Kingdom: BFI.

Nah, S. & Chung, D. (2012). When citizens meet both professional and citizen journalists: Social trust, media credibility, and perceived journalistic roles among online community news readers. *Journalism, 13*(8), 1–17.

Newman, N. (2009). *The Rise of Social Media and its Impact on Mainstream Journalism.* Oxford, United Kingdom: Reuters Institute for the Study of Journalism.

O'Beachain, D. & Polese, A., (2010). *The Colour Revolutions in the Former Soviet Republics: Successes and Failures.* Abingdon, United Kingdom: Routledge.

O'Neill, O. (2012, October 24). So, what is a free press? *The Guardian.*

Pannier, B. (2009). *Rethinking Kyrgyzstan's Tulip Revolution.* Retrieved from http://www.rferl.org/content/Rethinking_Kyrgyzstans_Tulip_Revolution/1807335.html

Papacharissi, Z. (2009). The Citizen is the Message: Alternative modes of civic engagement. In Z. Papacharissi (Ed.), *Journalism and Citizenship: New*

References

Agendas in Communication. Abingdon, United Kingdom: Routledge.

Parliament of Georgia. (2012). *Annual Statistics.* Retrieved from: www.parliament.ge

Pearce, K. & Kendzior, S. (2012). Networked authoritarianism and social media in Azerbaijan. *Journal of Communication, 62,* 283–98.

Perlmutter, D. (2008). *Blogwars,* Oxford, United Kingdom. Oxford University Press.

Recknagel, C. (2010). *Can Kyrgyzstan Become a Democracy in Russia's Backyard?* Retrieved from http://www.rferl.org/content/in_the_news_kyrgyzstan_russia_recknagel/2109083.html

Reese, S., Rutigliano, L., Hyun, K. & Jeong, J. (2009). Mapping the Blogosphere: Professional and citizen-based media in the global news arena. *Journalism, 8*(3), 235–51.

Reid. A. (1998). *Borderland: A journey through the history of Ukraine.* New York, NY: Basic Books.

Reporters without Borders (2012). *Press Freedom Index 2011 –12.* Retrieved from http://en.rsf.org/press-freedom-index-2011-2012,1043.html

Robakidze, N. (2011). Georgia: Immature media. *Caucasus Analytical Digest, 25,* 18 March.

Roberts, S. (2011). Postcode lottery: The future of cross-border media in post-devolution Wales. In D. Hutchinson and H. O'Donnell (Eds.). *Centres and Peripheries: Metropolitan and non-metropolitan journalism in the 21st century.* Newcastle upon Tyne, United Kingdom: Cambridge Scholars Publishing.

Rosen, J. (1999). *What are journalists for?* New Haven, CT: Yale University Press.

Sakr, N. (2013). *Transformations in Egyptian Journalism.* London, United Kingdom: I. B. Tauris.

Sambrook, R. (2006). *How the Net is Transforming News.* Retrieved from: http://news.bbc.co.uk/1/hi/technology/4630890.stm

Schudson, M. (2008). *Why Democracies Need an Unlovable Press.* Cambridge, United Kingdom: Polity.

Scotton, J. & Hachten, W. (2010). *New Media, New China.* Chichester, United Kingdom: Wiley-Blackwell.

Seib, P. (2002). *The Global Journalist: News and conscience in a world of conflict.* Lanahm, MD: Rowman and Littlefield.

Shafer, R. & Freedman, E. (2003). Press constraints as obstacles to establishing civil societies in Central Asia. *Journalism Studies, 10*(6), 851–69.

Shapovalova, N. (2011). *Ukraine's Managed Democracy.* Retrieved from http://www.fride.org/article/196/ukraine

Siapera, E. (2010). *Cultural Diversity and Global Media: The mediation of difference.* Chichester, United Kingdom: Wiley-Blackwell.

Siebert, F., Peterson, T. & Schramm, W. (1956). *Four Theories of the Press.* Urbana, IL: University of Illinois Press.

Smith, J. (2008). The limitations of blogging as a democratic practice. In T. Brabazon (Ed.), *The Revolution Will Not be Downloaded: Dissent in the digital age* (pp. 135–44). Cambridge, United Kingdom: Chandos Publishing.

Smith, K. & McConville, B. (2011). How the media marginalised the economic roots of the "Arab Spring". In J. Mair and R. Keeble (Eds.), *Mirage in the Desert? Reporting the "Arab Spring".* Bury St Edmunds, United Kingdom: Abramis.

Sparks, C. (2000). Media theory after the fall of European Communism. In J. Curran & M.-J. Park (Eds.), *De-*

Westernizing Media Studies (pp. 35-49). Abingdon, United Kingdom: Routledge.

Splichal, S. (2001). *Access Denied: Freedom of information in the information age.* Ames, IO: Iowa State University Press.

Splichal, S. & Sparks, C. (1994). *Journalists for the 21st Century: Tendencies of professionalization among first year students in 22 countries.* Norwood, NJ: Ablex.

Stromback, J. (2006). In search of a standard: Four models of democracy and their normative implications for journalism. *Journalism Studies, 6*(3), 331-45.

Suchman, L. & Jordan, B. (1992). Questions and answers in attitude surveys. In J. Tanner (Ed.), *Questions about Questions: Inquiries into the cognitive bases of surveys.* New York, NY: Russell Sage Foundation.

Tisdall, S. (2012, September 6). Pardoning of Azeri axe murderer raises tensions in the Caucasus. *The Guardian.*

Tuchman, G. (1978). *Making News.* New York, NY: Free Press.

Tunstall, J. (1971). *Journalists at Work.* London, United Kingdom. Constable Press.

United Nations Development Programme, 2012. *Country Profiles.* Retrieved from http://hdr.undp.org/en/countries/

The Week. (2012, March 3). Russia's Godfather: Is Putin running a gangster state?

World Economic Forum (2009). *Future of Journalism.* Retrieved in January 2010 from: www.weforum.org/pdf/GAC09/council/future_of_journalism/

Yerevan Press Club/Eastern Partnership Civil Society Forum (2011). *Media Landscapes of Eastern Partnership Countries.* Retrieved from www.ypc.am

Zolyan, M. (2010). Armenia. In D. O'Beachain, & A. Polese (Eds.), *The Colour Revolutions in the Former Soviet Republics: Successes and failures* (pp. 30–45). Abingdon, United Kingdom: Routledge.